HISTORICAL DISCOURSE

DELIVERED AT

AMHERST, N. H.,

ON THE

HUNDREDTH ANNIVERSARY

OF THE

Dedication of the Congregational Meeting-House,

BY THE PASTOR, J. G. DAVIS;

With sketches of Persons, Places, and Churches connected with the parish originally called Souhegan West, by Rev. A. Heald, S. H. Keeler, d.d., W. B. Towne, and D. F. Secomb, Esquires.

CONCORD, N. H.:
PRINTED BY THE REPUBLICAN PRESS ASSOCIATION.
1874.

AMHERST, Jan'y 26, 1874.

REV. DR. DAVIS:—

DEAR SIR,—The undersigned, having heard, with great satisfaction, your address commemorative of the one hundredth anniversary of the dedication of the church, and feeling that it should be put in form for preservation, earnestly request a copy for publication. A general desire is also expressed that the other valuable and interesting historical papers presented on that occasion may be printed with the discourse.

WM. A. MACK, H. E. WOODBURY,
DAVID FISK, WILLIAM PRATT,
LUTHER ELLIOTT, GEORGE DANFORTH,
AARON S. WILKINS, LEVI J. SECOMB,
GEO. W. BOSWORTH, Z. PERRY,
WILLIAM WETHERBEE.

AMHERST, Jan'y 27, 1874.

GENTLEMEN,—

In compliance with the request, so kindly expressed in your communication of the 26th, I submit the manuscript of my discourse to your disposal. The history is by no means complete, but, connected with the other papers that you propose to print under the same covers, will serve to keep alive the memory of the fathers, and thus quicken our gratitude to God for the great benefits conferred on us through their toils. With sincere esteem,

Yours, J. G. DAVIS.

To WILLIAM A. MACK, Esq.,
DAVID FISK, and others.

INTRODUCTION.

At a meeting of the Congregational Church, held Nov. 18, 1873, it was *Voted*, That the officers of the church, with Messrs. Levi J. Secomb and Jotham Hartshorn, be a committee to learn the wishes of citizens and church members, and ascertain whether it be expedient to observe the centennial of the dedication of the Congregational meeting-house, which occurred Jan. 19, 1774.

This committee met at Dea. Boylston's on the 25th, and decided that it is expedient to commemorate the dedication of the meeting-house, by a sermon and other appropriate exercises. It was subsequently determined to obtain sketches of the history of other churches which have been organized within the original limits of Amherst, as Milford, Mt. Vernon, and the Baptist and Methodist churches in town. Invitations were accordingly issued to pastors and others to furnish sketches of churches and deceased persons, with historical reminiscences suited to the occasion. Services were assigned to Sunday the 18th, and to Monday P. M. of the 19th of January, when the Methodist and Baptist societies, and the congregation from Mt. Vernon, united with the parent church in the worship of God in the old meeting-house.

The day was pleasant, and the sleighing excellent. The house was filled in every part, the aisles being furnished with extra seats.

The services of the morning opened with the doxology; invocation and reading of the scriptures by Rev. Mr. Ruland; prayer by Rev. Dr. Keeler; and singing 1st version of the 78th psalm,—

> "Let children hear the mighty deeds
> Which God performed of old"—*Tate & Brady*—

followed by the historical discourse, and prayer by Rev. Dr. Clark.

In the afternoon, after singing, and prayer by Rev. Mr. Heald, the salutations of the Methodist church were presented by Rev. Mr. Ruland in a cordial address, when Rev. Mr. Heald read his sketch of the Baptist church, and Dr. Keeler followed with the history of the church in Mt. Vernon.

The next day a large audience assembled in the Town Hall, at 1 o'clock P. M., the pastor of the Congregational church presiding. Rev. Mr. Heald offered prayer, when, in answer to a call from the chair, Hon. Wm. B. Towne gave a succinct history of the origin of the town of Milford, the organization of the church, and the services of its ministers.

In response to some remarks on the life and services of Daniel Campbell, Esq., one of the early settlers, Hon. Chas. H. Campbell, of Nashua, made a spirited address, abounding in choice anecdotes of the olden times, with grateful reminiscences of his ancestors and other respected citizens living in the neighborhood, establishing a claim* in behalf of the beautiful swell of land, which these men and their descendants have occupied for nearly a century, to be called the Moderator's Hill.

To this address succeeded the reading of interesting memorials of departed worthies and their times, by D. F. Secomb, Esq., of Concord, the son of John and brother of Levi J. Secomb, whose names are associated with long terms of service in important offices of the town.

The exercises were enlivened by cheery songs of the Apollo Club from Nashua. With a few earnest words from Dea. Boylston on the importance of making provision for the publication of a history of the town, the meeting was closed.

In the evening an organ concert was given by Geo. H. Ryder, of Boston, in which he was aided by Miss H. A. Russell, Mr. Merrill and his club, with the new instrument he had set up the week previous in the meeting-house. In concluding this sketch of the commemorative services, it is due to the authors of the several papers, now printed, to say that they are not as complete as they intended. The time for preparation was too short for extensive research or exhaustive treatment. In giving the sermon and sketches to the press, they are influenced by a desire to place these fragments of history in a form in which the materials may be preserved for the more thorough and comprehensive treatment which the good name and services of Amherst, Mt. Vernon, and Milford deserve.

---

* The claim is justified by the fact that six individuals, belonging to three families in that school district, have served as moderators at forty-one of the one hundred and fifteen annual town meetings held since the incorporation of the town. The same persons have served fifty-seven years on the board of selectmen, and represented the town fourteen years in the general court. They are Daniel Campbell, Daniel Campbell, Jr., Charles H. Campbell, John Secomb, Levi J. Secomb, and William A. Mack. S.

DISCOURSE.

JOHN 4:38. * * * OTHER MEN LABOURED, AND YE ARE ENTERED INTO THEIR LABORS.

HAGGAI 2:9. THE GLORY OF THIS LATTER HOUSE SHALL BE GREATER THAN OF THE FORMER, SAITH THE LORD OF HOSTS.

1 KINGS 8:57. THE LORD OUR GOD BE WITH US, AS HE WAS WITH OUR FATHERS. LET HIM NOT LEAVE US NOR FORSAKE US.

The great law of human progress, by which one generation enters on the labors of the preceding, and profits by its toil, has manifold illustrations. There was a preparation for the specific mission of the apostles, in the results wrought out by the counsels and experience of prophets and teachers who were commissioned before them. Each age gathers wisdom from the labors and researches of the preceding age. In every science, and in every art, we are constrained to acknowledge our indebtedness to the genius and industry of departed generations. So is it in respect to social customs, religious institutions, and all the essential features of our civilization. We have but taken up and carried forward the work which our fathers laid down.

One of the most important uses of historical discourses and commemorations is, to teach us what we owe to the past; to bring to mind the conditions of hardship and toil; the enterprise and patient industry by which our present prosperity was attained. Without some effort of this kind, by which we reproduce the lives and labors of those who have gone before us, we shall not adequately value the heritage on which we have entered, and by which we are so richly endowed. The event which we commemorate this day is not in itself so remarkable as to deserve special notice. The dedication of a house, erected for public worship at this day, has seldom any wide interest beyond the gratification of those who are to be accommodated beneath its roof. But this was not the sentiment a hundred years ago. The erection of a meeting-house, in the early history of the New England towns, was memorable as the result of a purpose to honor God in circumstances of hardship and destitution. It was accomplished amidst difficulties, and with an outlay of time and labor which was a heavy tax on the inhabitants. The building of lofty height, which was usually planted on some eminence, was the exponent of an idea that entered into and fashioned the character of the people. It was not merely an expression of religious feeling, but an expression of the principle that religion is to be maintained by the keeping of Sabbaths, and regular public instruction in the doctrines of the Bible. When we learn that the grantees of the Narragansett township were required "to pass such rules and orders as will effectually oblige them to settle sixty families, at least, in each township, with a learned and orthodox ministry, within the space of seven years from the date of this grant," and when we learn that "if the said grantees shall not effectually settle the said number of families in each township, and also lay out a lot for the first settled minister, one for the ministry, and one for the school in each of said townships, they shall have no advantage of, but forfeit their respective grants,"—it is obvious that, in the minds of those legislators, education and religion were held essential to the well-being of society; that in peopling a township there was a necessity of providing for the education of children, and for the religious culture and worship of all the inhabitants. If these ideas could not be realized, they were not disposed to encourage new settlements.

It has been alleged that the members of the Massachusetts

government, in making these grants, "were influenced more by motives of policy than those of benevolence," as "they wished to retain property in the lands, in case the jurisdiction was taken away." That considerations of this nature were active in promoting these grants may be admitted. To suppose that these settlements would be undertaken without any prospect of personal advantage, is to assume a superhuman virtue in our ancestors to which they made no claims. The commendable feature of the transaction is, that, having in view the acquisition of landed property, they did not overlook nor neglect the higher conditions that respected the service of God and the spiritual welfare of the emigrants. The persons to whom the grant No. 3, at Souhegan West, was made, lived in Essex county, Massachusetts; and, as few of the original proprietors came into New Hampshire, the harmony of their action in accepting the trust is the more noticeable.

It is with some diffidence* that I attempt to describe the movements of the first settlers. The early landmarks have disappeared; and it is not easy to reproduce the scenes in which they planted their habitations. To men employed in subjugating the forests, clearing lots, making roads, and rearing log houses, there was no leisure, and little disposition, to make careful records of the place and progress of their occupations. The first settlement in the territory was made in 1734, the same year in which the proprietors held their first meeting at Salem Village (now Danvers), Mass. The emigrants were mainly from the towns of Essex county: at a later period valuable accessions to the population came from Middlesex county. On taking possession of the township in 1735,—after a plan which distributed the soil into

* The author desires to acknowledge his indebtedness to Dea. E. D. Boylston for the use of original letters and other valuable MSS. from his private collections, with the loan of the "Proprietors' Records" belonging to Hon. C. H. Campbell. His thanks are due to D. F. Secomb, Esq., of Concord, for many anecdotes of the early inhabitants, with copies of papers from the archives of the state. Edward Spalding, M. D., and William B. Towne, Esq., have also aided him by personal recollections and other information.

three sections, with sub-divisions into lots of sixty acres each,—the proprietors vote "to lay out a place whereon to erect a meeting-house;" and, in August of the same year, they also vote "to build." A meeting-house would be of little use without worshippers. We accordingly read of appropriations, to induce people to move hither and take up lands. At first, a grant is made of £6 to each settler on clearing two acres of land, and the completion of a house 18x18, and 7 feet stud,—a grant subsequently increased to £20 to actual settlers. This will explain the delay in executing the earlier votes. The way was not prepared. Openings must be made in the forests, the soil broken, and crops raised, before men and materials could be had for the house of worship. In February of 1737–38, the subject is brought up anew, and they decide "to build a house forty-five feet in length, thirty-five in width, and twenty-two feet stud,"—a structure of generous proportions for that period, answering in its area to one half of the room we now occupy. They proposed to cover the outside and erect a pulpit within twelve months, and £3 per right was assessed on the proprietors to pay for the same. This house, which was located on the rising ground at the junction of the roads then leading to Bedford and through the west parish to New Boston, was actually raised in May of 1739, when Capt. Ebenezer Raimond was instructed to provide entertainment for the raising,—a laborious and somewhat dangerous undertaking. In that year, the inhabitants were authorized to draw £20 from the treasury "towards their having the word of God preached among them for the next six mos.," which was supplemented by another grant of £20 in July, to pay for preaching till next March, "if they bring the men's names that preached ten days,"—a somewhat ambiguous condition, but intended, I assume, to prevent a misapplication of the money, as, in December, they adopted a different rule, by which "50 shillings was voted for each Sabbath they shall have preaching among them." Without certain information, it is doubtful whether preaching was maintained with much regularity. According to a tradition, the thirteenth family that settled in the township was that of Mr. (afterward Rev.) Daniel Wilkins (Harvard col., 1736). He came with his wife from Middleton, Mass., in compliance with the solicitations of the families that came here from that place and vicinity. This was in 1740; and in April of the following year, the proprietors concur in the action of the settlers in desiring Mr. Wilkins to become their minister, "provided we can agree with him for salary and settlement." The negotiations resulted favorably, and in August they vote to accept the report of the committee "that was chosen to treat with Mr. Daniel Wilkins about salary and settlement." At the same meeting a committee was chosen "to take care of the ordination," with instructions "not to exceed £40, but as much less as they can." This committee was also to designate "the time and advise the clerk, that he may put it into the newspaper." On the 22d of September, 1741, the church was organized, and six males, including the pastor elect, subscribed the covenant, which, with slight alterations, abides in use unto this day. The covenant contained six articles, presenting a concise and admirable statement of Christian duty.* No confession of faith was required; and, after repeated inquiries, I have never been able to learn at what time, or by whose counsel, the articles of faith now prefixed to the covenant were adopted. On the next day, September 23d, Rev. Daniel Wilkins was ordained pastor, by a council of five ministers and fourteen lay delegates, of whom the church in Middleton, from which Mr. Wilkins came, sent five, and the church in Dunstable three. Rev. Nathaniel Henchman, of Lynn, was moderator of the coun-

---

* The only rules adopted by the church besides this covenant, for more than thirty years, are the following: In 1750, "*Voted*, That no persons should have the privilege of baptism for their children, without a certificate from the church to which they belonged." In 1757, "*Voted*, That the satisfaction for all public offences shall be equal to the crimes."

cil, and Rev. Stephen Chase, of Lynn, preached the sermon. The prayer of ordination was probably offered by Rev. Andrew Peters, of Middleton,—the other parts of the service falling to Rev. James Osgood, of Wenham, Mass., and Rev. Josiah Swan, of Dunstable. Immediately after the ordination, six females were admitted to church membership, Sarah Wilkins, the wife of the pastor, being of the number. But where, we ask, were the services of installation held? Did the people gather in some opening of the forest, amidst "the sounding aisles of the dim woods?" Did the fathers find a sanctuary in the unfinished apartment of a log house? Possibly they found accommodation "in the convenient house of entertainment" which Capt. Richard Mower was to build, in consideration of lot No. 25, of which he was to have sure title; perhaps a shelter was found within the frame of the meeting-house, which might have been covered with boughs or boards for the occasion. We cannot answer the question, concerning which we may well be curious, as somewhat to our amazement we read,* more than two years after the installation, "that the committee to be chosen get the meeting-house boarded, and the floor laid, the body seats made up, and the pulpit made, and the doors made and hung, as soon as can be." In February following (1744), they vote "that they will do something towards finishing the meeting-house, viz., to clapboard it, and make the window frames, crown and glaze them, to point the ground-pointing, and prime the flew-boards, window frames, sashes, and doors; and in case there is not an Indian war next fall, to lath and plaster the meeting-house, as the committee shall think best." These votes were doubtless carried into effect during the next summer, so far as to exclude the wind and snow, as a meeting of the proprietors is called at the meeting-house early in the year 1745. But what a picture these votes suggest to the imagination, of the privations

---

* Proprietor's Records, Oct. 18th, 1743.

and hardship of the early inhabitants. If the ordination took place on the site of the meeting-house, they had at the best only a roof over their heads. The population of the township could not have exceeded twenty families, and they over-worked by clearing lands, building barns, houses, fences, and making pathways through the forests. Money was scarce, and the currency continually depreciating. Yet they endured hardness as good soldiers,—the pastor giving an example to his flock, putting his hand to the axe and the plough, sharing all the exposures of his brethren. And these exposures were such as might dishearten brave men. On their scattered farms they were much annoyed by wild beasts. Wolves prowled about their pathways, and preyed upon their sheep; at times the bears caused them much trouble; but these perils were soon aggravated by apprehensions of more deadly foes.

Fortunately for the townships lying back from the Merrimack river, the Indian population had not been numerous. Whether wasted by disease, or driven back by earlier conflicts, the region which the settlers entered had been deserted by the aborigines. Before the announcement of war between France and England, the allies of the former had been excited to hostilities by emissaries of the same power that provoked the expedition against Louisbourg. Working southward from the Canadas, the Indians hovered about the infant settlements, capturing and slaying the inhabitants, and burning their dwellings wherever they were unprotected. In this exigency the inhabitants of Souhegan West procured ammunition, and proceeded to fortify their dwellings and make provision for defence against the assailants. They also held a meeting at the house of their pastor, in which they unanimously agreed that Daniel Wilkins, in the name and behalf of the settlers of this plantation, should represent to the Governor and Council of the Province of New-Hampshire "our distressing circumstances, on account of our exposure to the French and Indian enemy." They needed defence while about their work. The petition prepared by Rev. Mr. Wilkins was presented at Portsmouth, June 22, 1744, and—

"Humbly sheweth the said town has been settled by his majesty's subjects about nine years, and a gospel minister ordained almost three years; that the settlers have an eye at enlarging his majesty's dominions, by going into the wilderness, as well as their own interest; that some thousands of pounds has been spent in clearing and cultivating the lands there, and vast sums in building houses, barns, and fences, besides much time and expense in building fortifications, by His Excellency the Governor's order.

"That the breaking up of the settlement will not only ruin the memorialists, but greatly disserve his majesty's interest by encouraging his enemies to encroach on his deserted settlements, and be also hurtful to the province by contracting the borders and drawing the war nearer the capital.

"That it was by a long and importunate intercession of this province (and not of the memorialists' seeking) that they are left under the immediate care of this government, which they conceive gives them so much the better right to its protection.

"That as war is already declared against France, and a rupture with the Indians hourly expected, your memorialists, unless they have speedy help, will soon be obliged to forsake their town, how disserviceable soever it may be to the crown, dishonorable to the government, hurtful to the province, and ruinous to ourselves.

"Wherefore, your memoralists most humbly supplicate Your Excellency, the Honorable Council, and House of Representatives to take the premises into your wise and mature consideration, and to grant them such reasonable relief as may enable them to subsist in the war and secure against the ravages and devastations of a bloodthirsty and merciless enemy: and your memorialists, as in duty bound, will ever pray."

In his argument Mr. Wikins insists that the danger is imminent, and adroitly reminds the government that it was not of their choice that they were dependent on its protection.

In answer to this petition, scouts were provided for this place, and Salem Canada (now Lyndeborough) on the west. The following year, at a meeting of the proprietors at Chelmsford, Mass., a motion was carried imposing "an obligation to get sixty families to settle in the township immediately, according to the act of Massachusetts." But with all their efforts, it was difficult persuading men to move up into the wilderness, where, as yet, there was no smith to sharpen their tools, no mill to grind their corn, and the dread of the Indians required the inhabitants to keep armed. In May of 1747, the government having withdrawn its protection, a new petition is forwarded to His Excellency Benning Wentworth, which showeth that the plantation contained thirty-five families, and about fifty-eight men upwards of sixteen years old:

"That when we began our settlement we apprehended no danger of our ever being a frontier, there being at that time so many above us begun and obligated to fulfil the conditions of the Massachusetts grants, which occasioned us to settle scattering, only regarding the advantage of good and compact farms.

"That the difficulty of war happening so early on our settlements, and the defenceless condition they were in, has obliged them all, viz., Peterborough, Salem Canada, New Boston, and Hillsborough (so-called), entirely to draw off,—as well as the forts on Connecticut river left naked,—whereby we are now left as much exposed as any of the frontiers on Merrimack river.

"That the first year of the present war we were favored with a scout from this province (which we thankfully acknowledge), and Salem Canada with another, which was equally serviceable to us. Since that time both Salem Canada and this place has had a guard from the Massachusetts till the winter passed, together with our inhabitants keeping a constant scout (though much impoverished thereby).

"That this encouragement has occasioned our venturing here till now.

"That, as we are now left without either scout or guard, apprehend we are in imminent danger, yet loath to yield ourselves such an easy prey to our enemies, or suffer ruin by leaving our improvements waste,—one whereof we have no reason to think but must unavoidably be our lot unless the government compassionately grants us protection."

This application for soldiers to protect the inhabitants is signed by twenty-three persons; among whom appear the names of Wilkins, Shepard, Peabody, Hutchinson, Cheever, Howard, Hartshorn, Bixbe, Seetown, Bradford, Ellenwood, Clark, Towne, Lyon, Stiles. These were among the earliest land-owners; and their descendants continue with us unto this day. The hardships of the first settlers were not readily mitigated, as we may infer from their continued apprehension of attacks from the Indians, and the necessity of maintaining guards and scouts and ranging companies at suitable rallying points in the territory. Certain houses were entrenched by stockades, and the walls made bullet-proof for the shelter of women and children. There were seven of these garrison houses, at which a watch was maintained at different periods. The Rev. Mr. Wilkins occupied one of the garrison houses, and took his turn in the watch which was maintained by the citizens whenever an invasion was threatened. For months in succession it was the habit of the men to carry their muskets to the meeting-house, to be within reach and ready to be lifted should an alarm be given during the service. The vigilance they practised reminds us of the precautions taken by Nehemiah against Sanballat and Tobiah, the Arabians and the Ammonites,—in all which they were encouraged by the example of the pastor, who came to the place of worship having his gun in one hand and his Bible in the other. Both implements of his warfare were taken into the pulpit. The Indians frequently came hither with hostile intentions; but the settlers usually obtained information of their designs, and no one was killed or taken captive from Amherst. According to a family tradition,* a party under the lead of Dea. Hobbs† fell in with the Indians, on a Sunday morning, when a smart fight ensued, in which Hobbs displayed remarkable courage and prudence, bringing off his men with few wounded,—none mortally,—while they were positive that several Indians were killed. The result of this encounter was to give the men great reputation for bravery in circumstances of danger. The minister and others used to speak of the exploit with great satisfaction. On the other hand, it is reported that the Indians said that "Souhegan deacon no very good,—he fight Sabba day." The danger and annoyance from the Indians, which Farmer‡ assigns to a period commencing ten years later, at the outbreak of the French and Indian war in western Virginia, in 1754, belongs in fact to this earlier period. In the expeditions sent out at the latter date for the defence of the colonies and the conquest of Canada, the inhabitants of Souhegan West shared with the neighboring towns in furnishing their proportion of soldiers; and on the declaration of peace in 1763, they shared in the prevailing sentiment of joy and gratitude at the relief.

To return to the immediate interests of the parish. It is certain that the intentions of the proprietors in completing the meeting-house were not carried into full effect in 1751,

---

* Contained in a letter of Philip C. Wilkins, grandson of the minister.

† "January the sixth, 1742, the church voted that there be five sacraments within a year,—the first, the first Sabbath in March, the second, the first Sabbath in May," and thence bi-monthly. The last sacrament was observed on the first Sabbath of November. "At the same time the church chose Humphrey Hobbs deacon." This office "he resigned in 1744, and James Cochran was chosen in his room." Dea. Hobbs seems to have left town soon after, as he had command of a company of rangers employed in the defence of the settlements on Connecticut river, at Charlestown No. 4. He had the courage and capacity of a true soldier, and is probably mentioned as —— Hobbs, captain, in Report of Adj't-General N. H., Military History, vol. ii, p. 158.

‡ N. H. Historical Collections, vol. v, p. 88.

thirteen years after the vote fixing the site and dimensions of the building, and eleven years after the frame was set up, —a delay which has its justification in their poverty and the pressure of adverse circumstances. In succeeding years we find votes for the assignment of seats, or "dignifying the house," as it was called in Massachusetts; also, petitions from some who wished to sit together "for the better control of their families in worship;" requests that the "quiresters might sit in company to improve the psalmody or religious singing." On one page, the young men petition that they "may make seats on the beams in front of the meeting-house,"—probably the unfinished gallery,—and others of a similar import, aiming at better accommodations. On the first application, these requests were usually negatived; but better opinions prevailed, and, in the progress of years, families were allowed to sit in companies, the singers were brought together, and pew ground was assigned to those who would pay for it,—the money being applied "to finishing up the meeting-house."

At the best, the arrangements of the first house of worship must have been inconvenient, and when any improvements were attempted, difficulties would be suggested which usually defeated these designs. On the incorporation of the town, there were fresh reasons for postponement, as the question then arose "whether the house belonged to the town or to the proprietors,"—the conflict of ownership affording sufficient reason to hinder any outlay of money. On what terms, or at what date the ownership was adjusted, I cannot determine. The town at length held possession; and these delays, with the consequent vexations, may have served a useful purpose in preparing the community to build another and more commodious house of worship.

Before I speak of the origin of the new house, the building in which we are now assembled, it will be of service to notice some of the changes which had transpired, affecting the prosperity of the township. In 1741, the inhabitants, much against their wishes, had come under the jurisdiction of the province of New Hampshire; and in 1760, on the 18th day of January, one hundred and fourteen years ago this day, a charter was granted, by which the town was incorporated by the name Amherst. The population was sufficient to secure a representative to the general court. Mr. Wilkins was chosen minister of the town, with a salary of £47 10*s*. sterling money of Great Britain, or its equivalent in the currency or products of the country.

The tedious and exhausting war with the French had terminated successfully in the conquest of Canada. Agriculture had revived; domestic arts and manufactures began to engage the attention of the people; and a more equitable and easy administration of justice was now demanded. Hitherto the town of Amherst lay wholly on the north side of the Souhegan river,—the town of Monson, which was situated between this place and Hollis, lying on the south. For some cause not fully understood at this day, there was an antipathy to the people of Monson, which led the people of Amherst to reject all proposals for annexation. They even refused them a place in the meeting-house, "unless they would severally be assessed to support the minister;" but in 1770, about the time of the final distribution of the proprietors' lands by the action of the general court, Monson was divided between Amherst and Hollis. By this arrangement a strip of land, some two miles in breadth and six in length,—say thirteen square miles,—was added to the territory, and several families, needing church accommodations, to the population. In the meantime a lively competition was started among the townships of this region in hope of obtaining the county seat, whenever the expected division of the state, by shires or counties, should be established. Petitions, counter-petitions, and remonstrances were sent from the places most interested to the assembly. A remonstrance, which has attracted special notice, went from this place, written by Mr. Wilkins, against making Merrimack the shire town. The precise influence of these efforts cannot now be determined; but on the formation of Hillsborough county, Amherst became the shire town. In anticipation of this decision, a new importance was given to the place. Men of enterprise seeking business, and professional gentlemen moving hither, the town voted "to build a new meeting-house, to be located on the training field, seventy-five by fifty feet,"—a huge, barn-like structure; also, voted "to raise £150 lawful money towards defraying expenses of said building."

This plan was subsequently modified by a change which diminished the size of the structure, and provided somewhat for its embellishment. They voted to contract the dimensions, by taking five feet from the length and five from the breadth; to have a porch at one end, and a steeple, with belfry and weathercock, at the other. This was the approved pattern at that period. Previously, if a meeting-house had tower and bell, the spire rose from the centre of the roof, and the bell-rope came to the floor in the middle aisle.

A measure of such importance as the erection of a new meeting-house was not carried without much excitement and debate. The opposition was strong,—but not unanimous, or the project would have failed. The interests of "Chestnut Hill folks and of Monson folks" were of course antagonistic. People in the north-west part of the town grumbled at the prospect of paying towards a new house in which they were not to worship, and the district embracing Shepard's mills was thoroughly disaffected. Petitions crowded upon the selectmen, and a town-meeting was called November 6, 1770, for the purpose "of annulling or modifying the previous votes, and see if the town would not consent to repair the old house;" but the majority were united and unyielding, and they voted "to ratify, establish, and confirm the previous action of the town, and refused to repair the old meeting-house." Then followed a series of meetings to change the location; but they were ineffectual. The objection, that the site was too wet at certain seasons of the year, did not prevail ; and the alleged superiority "of a location near the united roads for good underpinning and freedom from water" did not convince those who preferred the site on the training field. The building committee, who supervised the work, consisting of Robert Read, Samuel McKean, Archelaus Towne, John Shepard, Jr., and Moses Nichols, adopted "the plan of the old North Church in Concord," so pleasantly associated in our minds with the fruitful ministry of Rev. Dr. McFarland. The house was set broad side to the south, with folding doors opening from the broad aisle on an ample pavement, flanked by two horse-blocks. The work was commenced in the spring of 1771, the town manifesting its hospitality by voting ample supplies of victuals and drink for all who should attend the raising. The occasion brought together a great company, strong men and agile, besides many spectators. The committee of entertainment must have managed with some discretion, not exceeding their instructions, that, with such powers to distribute New England rum among the thirsty crowd, the huge timbers of this massive frame were set in their places without serious injury to life or limb. The master-builder was Dea. Ephraim Barker, who had a wide reputation as a skilful mechanic.

It illustrates the habits of this period to learn that the raising was followed by athletic games and feats of strength. The iron-sided men, who were present from far and near, must not separate without an exhibition of their strength and agility. On this occasion there was a wrestling match ; and the minister's son, afterwards Dea. Samuel Wilkins, ran a short distance on a wager, " carrying on his shoulders the chairman of the building committee, who, like Eli of old, was fat and heavy —probably the heaviest man then in town."

In December the town voted " to finish the outside of the meeting-house, clapboard and glaze the same, complete the steeple, and lay floors." One hundred and sixty pounds were granted to pay the expenses thus far.

For various reasons the work proceeded slowly. The

people were poor, and serious dissensions impaired their strength. Portions of the town were dissatisfied, and consequently reluctant to pay their taxes.

Other matters of grave concern were pressing on their attention. The people of New Hampshire, in sympathy with the citizens of Massachusetts, had long regarded, with mingled feelings of dread and indignation, the acts of the British parliament. The course of adverse legislation, the stamp and tea tax, which led sagacious men like Adams and Franklin to anticipate a separation of the colonies from the mother country, and the assertion of their independence, had now reached a point when open resistance was freely talked. Remembering the persistent encroachments of England upon their liberties, the people welcomed the idea of making common cause with other colonies in plans of mutual coöperation and defence. The discipline of the French and Indian war had begotten a thoroughly military spirit in this part of the land. There was no lack of courage ; but the poverty of the citizens was undeniable. Whence could they obtain the materials of war, the arms and ammunition, requisite to contend with such a power as Great Britain ? These questions were already holding the thoughts of multitudes. We detect their presence in the action taken at the town-meetings. In September, following the dedication of this meeting-house, by vote of the town, a building is constructed for the safe storing of powder. It was substantial, being made of chestnut logs hewn twelve inches square, and covered with plaster. If any are impatient of the delays attending the completion of the building, let them consider that the minds of the people were sorely distracted by local dissensions, which found adjustment only in the formation of two other parishes or townships, besides the uncertainty and excitement attending the ripening apprehension of conflict with Great Britain.

Of the services at the dedication we have no minute information. It had not been the custom in New England to set apart places of worship by a solemn public consecration.

The first house was never formally dedicated. On this occasion several ministers were present as the guests of Mr. Wilkins. We have no record of the names, but the neighboring ministers might be expected, *e. g.*, Livermore of Wilton, Goodrich of Lyndeborough, Kidder of Dunstable, Emerson of Hollis, Burnap of Merrimack, to whom he extended the right hand of fellowship two years before, and possibly some visitors from the older towns of Essex county, Mass. A sermon was preached by the pastor, in which he is said to have given a history of the church and the early transactions of the settlement. Could we but recover the MS., what light it would throw upon the habits, the religious doctrines and worship, of the first inhabitants! We have no question of the genuineness of their faith and of the sincerity of their love. A people moving into the forests, to clear for themselves homesteads in the solitudes of the wilderness, do not take on themselves the burden of building meeting-houses and sustaining ministers without deep convictions of the value of the gospel. But it would gratify our reverent curiosity to know more exactly how these men felt, what operated to cheer and what to depress them, what books they read, what tunes they sung, how they fared in the winter* without the regular service. But the records are very scanty. In gratitude to God, they set down the names of the children as they were baptized; but of their own toils, their prayers, their self-denial, and their achievements, they say nothing. The strength of their devotion may be inferred from their sacrifices to maintain worship and their belief of the truth, from the unfaltering purpose to train up their children under the instructions of an orthodox ministry.

In Dec. 4, 1771, before the new meeting-house was ready for occupation, on the question of giving the old meeting-

---

* From letters and various memorandums, it appears that before the forests were cut off the snow accumulated in such quantities that the roads in winter were impassable. The people went abroad on rackets; and contracts for the delivery of fuel and lumber provided that the same should be drawn on the March crust, when teams could usually move in any direction, with no obstruction save buildings and trees.

house to the county for a court-house, we read,—"Secondly, voted, and hereby do give, grant, and forever quit claim all our right, title, interest, claim, and property in and unto our old meeting-house in said Amherst, to the justices of the court of general sessions of the peace for said county, for the use of said county, reserving to ourselves the privilege of congregating in said house from time to time, as we shall see meet, for the space of two years, to commence from this time, without having it made inconvenient for that purpose; reserving to ourselves the right to remove the pulpit out of the house at any time within the two years aforesaid: *Provided*, nevertheless, and the above vote is upon this condition, that the justices aforesaid cause a new county jail to be erected within one hundred and sixty rods of said house, as it now stands; otherwise, the above vote and every clause therein contained to be void."

The conditions prescribed by the town were accepted, the jail erected on the spot where stands the old county house, and the first house of worship was transferred from the use of the church to the service of the state.* At the expiration of the two years, as we have seen, the new house was dedicated to the worship of God. The floor of the house or pew ground was subsequently sold at auction to the highest bidder, the purchasers erecting pews at their own cost, under the direction of a committee, who were instructed to have "three tiers of pews on the south side, one on the north, two tiers at the east end, and two tiers at the west end; alleys to be between the pews and seats, and between the pews:" a description which becomes intelligible when we learn that below the pulpit were seats for the deacons, and, across the aisle from them, rows of seats for the aged men, the fathers of the congregation. The pews intended for families were eight or ten feet square, surmounted by a

* In 1789 this building was removed from the original site to the plain, and, before it was quite finished, burned by the fire of an incendiary. *Memoir of Joshua Atherton, p. 31.*

rail, which was supported by small wooden balusters, through which the children could peer out and get a view of the galleries and the inmates of adjoining pews. The pulpit or "imprisonment" was built high up against the north wall, having a narrow stair-case on the left or west side, "and a door that shut the preacher in." Over the sacred desk, and hanging from the ceiling by an iron rod, was the sounding-board, an object of wonder and curious speculation to all the juvenile hearers, who were mentally asking what would happen if it should fall upon the minister. "The seats," we are told, "were not on golden hinges hung," and as they were lifted, when the congregation rose, the uprising and down-sitting of the people were accompanied with a crash and clatter not unlike the discharge of musketry on training days. The pews also had arm-rests and leaning-boards for the support of weary heads. When these bars were lifted, being set upright, something formidable might have been anticipated from this bristling movement. The house had galleries on three sides, supported by smooth, substantial wooden columns, which were painted in imitation of marble. Against the walls was a tier of pews, in front of which were seats for strangers, for domestics, a reserved bench for the blacks, and in front of the preacher a section of the gallery was set apart for the singers. The rich and poor met together in the sanctuary, and united in recognizing the Lord their maker; but it was not in harmony with the ideas of that day that they should sit together;—hence the divisions, arrangements, and orders of which I have spoken. The churches were democratic in their theories of church government and membership, but they were not yet emancipated from the force of hereditary customs. The various arrangements for the accommodation of worshippers were not completed at once. Several years elapsed before the house was furnished throughout with seats in the style which you associate with the palmy days of Dr. Lord's ministry. In the ordering of the house of God, changes were esteemed dangerous innovations, and the proposition to assign seats to the singers, "for the better regulation of psalmody," came before the town several times without approval. The affairs of the country had the precedence of all other matters and things,—"the acts of the grand congress at Philadelphia," the business of providing soldiers, procuring salt and powder, designating committees of safety, and choosing delegates to state and county conventions. These duties, together with measures of relief for soldiers' families, and safeguards against the intrigues of tories, gave the people sufficient occupation. The inevitable anxiety attending the exhausting conflict was aggravated by differences of opinion respecting the principles and conduct of public men, and the consequent exasperation and bitterness of feeling did not subside with the close of the war. Contrary to what might have been our expectation, the return of peace brought no relief from political strife. The questions that became prominent respected the relation of the new states to one another and the general government. Local questions of civil rights, the jurisdiction of courts and magistrates, also required adjustment; the choice of rulers, and the selection of delegates to settle the powers and duties of state officers and frame a constitution, were imperative affairs. Almost all of these subjects were brought before the citizens in their primary meetings. The importance which they attached to them is evinced in the appointment of large committees for counsel and correspondence, and frequent adjournments to wait further information.

Meanwhile, Pastor Wilkins growing infirm and needing an assistant, the duty of supplying the pulpit was intrusted to a committee in 1776, who were to employ "such young preachers as they chose." Soon after, the congregation were evidently interested in Mr. Sweatland, and wished to secure his services. In 1778, liberal proposals were made to Mr. John Blydenburg to settle as colleague with Mr. Wilkins; but without success. Similar propositions were offered Mr. Edmund Foster, which he declined. In the autumn of 1779, a call was extended to Rev. Jeremiah Barnard,* of Bolton, Mass., on similar terms. He was willing to accept; but the ordination did not occur till the following March, when the sermon was preached by Rev. Zabdiel Adams of Lunenburg, Bridge of Chelmsford giving the charge, and Emerson of Hollis the right hand of fellowship. The opposition to his settlement was in part personal, some of the hearers preferring a more positive style of preaching; for it was manifest that Mr. Barnard did not present the doctrines, as they were called, with much prominence and pungency. But this consideration had less weight than territorial interests. For obvious reasons, the settlers on the green hills of the north-west desired the benefits of a ministry nearer home. They lived remote from the first meeting-house, and the second was yet half a mile farther off by the travelled way. They had entered into agreements to support Mr. Wilkins, and to pay other charges until they should be set off as the second parish. Of course they were determined not to share in additional burdens. On the other hand, it was to be said that the population of the town (1,428 in '75) was not too large for one parish. The majority did not wish the territory divided; their local importance, their wealth or numbers, diminished;—and the import of their successive votes, in answer to the petitions from the north-west, make it clear that they would not let that people go if they could help it. The struggle was carried on for years in various shapes, sometimes involving litigation in which the majority were not always successful; and in September, 1780, only six months after Mr. Barnard's ordination, the second church in Amherst was formed, and the ecclesiastical strife, in that direction, ended. From that date the town acted as a parish.

The efforts that had been made for the formation of a third parish in the south-west part of the town, which resulted in the organization of a church in 1788, also originated

---

* Mr. B. was the son of Robert Barnard, of Bolton, Mass., where he was born Feb 28, 1750. He graduated at Harvard college in 1773.

in pleas of greater convenience for the inhabitants; but the arguments were not so obviously just; and subsequent events incline one to the opinion that the movement had in it "an element of carnal policy." The town of Amherst owed much to the ministry of Rev. Mr. Wilkins. We have no statistics from which to deduce exact statements respecting the results of his ministry. From all that I can gather, he was a man of great simplicity and purity of character. Having an intelligent and well-balanced mind, he made himself the guardian and friend of his people. In their perils and discouragements he shared in their distresses, and bade them take heart. Twice, probably, in the history of the plantation, his counsels prevented their abandoning the territory. He must have been patient, and of a scholarly turn of mind; he must have been diligent in pastoral labors, teaching them by families, or he would not have instructed the people so thoroughly. He was evidently wise and kind, or he would not have held so large a place in their affections. In person, he was a thick-set but well-formed man, of ruddy countenance and genial speech. At the age of sixty-three his mental faculties became impaired, and he was unequal to the duties of the ministry; but the people cared for him thoughtfully, seeking his presence and services in their families as long as he could venture abroad. When he died the town assumed the whole expense of his burial, and honored his grave by a monument on which they inscribed in glowing words their admiration of his virtues, and their grateful remembrance of his laborious services as their minister.

The years following the close of the revolution were marked by a general decline in the tone of religious feeling. Infidelity prevailed widely among men of wealth and culture. The claims of piety were openly derided, and the fashionable sentiment favored a thoughtless and jovial manner of life. The minds of men were agitated by political questions, in which pastors and churches were often involved. The formation of the national and state constitutions, the inauguration of new officers, the interpretation of their powers and duties under the new administration, the adoption of a better system of finance, the introduction of new industries, and the necessity of repairing the wastes of the war, engrossed the attention of the people. The concerns of religion were very much crowded aside. Amherst, being the shire town, the seat of the courts, in what had become a thickly settled portion of the state, became the resort of lawyers, politicians, and patriots. The Hillsborough county bar was distinguished for the talent and legal ability of its members. The sessions of the court occupied several weeks of the year, and the business was of such importance as to bring hither the foremost lawyers of the state. The town also became the centre of a large and lucrative trade, and the population in 1790 reached two thousand three hundred and sixty-nine. As a consequence of this prosperity, aristocratic tastes and customs prevailed,—a fondness for gaming, dancing, and convivial entertainments, which did not favor sobriety or a serious tone of thought.

There was little in Mr. Barnard's preaching to disturb the prevailing sentiment. He was an amiable man, made his house attractive to the young people, and in various ways contributed to the good order and social culture of the community. His sympathies were not with the Calvinistic school of ministers, and as years advanced his chosen associates were of the less evangelical type. During the period of his active ministry two hundred and fifty-three persons were admitted to full communion, an average of seven per annum. Several others owned the covenant, as it was called, and had their children baptized. This is not the place to discuss the merits of that custom; but the erroneous practice was discontinued before the settlement of his successor. At this day it is not easy to pronounce judgment on the actual fruits of Mr. Barnard's ministry. He entered the field while the land was overshadowed by the war-cloud of the revolution, and his retirement from active duties was close upon the conclusion of the war of 1815. How far these events contributed to the predominant political tone of his sermons I cannot determine. The dissatisfaction felt by many who loved a more discriminating gospel was doubtless increased by this patriotic zeal for the federal side in politics. It has also operated to the prejudice of Mr. Barnard's ministry that, like Mr. Wilkins, he lived many years after he became infirm and quite unequal to public service, and during that time he was not altogether in sympathy with his earnest and successful colleagues. Unless we assume that Amherst was unusually favored in the additions to its population from abroad, the ministry of Mr. Barnard must have been of much practical force, or the people would not, by such majorities, have welcomed a preacher like his successor. Mr. Barnard lived to the advanced age of eighty-four, dying January 15, 1835.* We now reach a period which is well known by tradition to this generation. Your fathers worshipped in this house, and some of their number joined in the call by which Mr. Nathan Lord, of South Berwick, Me., became pastor. The vote of the church is said to have been unanimous, and the town concurred with them in their action. At the ordination, Dr. McFarland preached the sermon; Rev. David McGregor offered the prayer of consecration; the senior pastor gave the charge; and Rev. Dr. Moore gave the right hand of fellowship.†

Mr. Lord had very positive and distinct views of the duties of the ministry, and he brought to the performance of those duties a vigorous and well-trained mind. His preaching was marked by clearness of statement, neatness and precision of style, and a prevailing seriousness

* For list of Mr. Barnard's published writings, see Farmer's History (New Hampshire Historical Society's Collection), vol. v, p. 115.

† The sermon, charge, and fellowship of the churches, delivered on that occasion, were published by R. Boylston, Amherst, 1816. Dr. Lord, son of Hon. John Lord, was born at South Berwick, Me., 28th of November, 1792; graduated Bowdoin College, 1809; Andover Seminary, 1815; pastor, 1816–1828; president Dartmouth college, 1828–1863; died at Hanover 9th of September, 1870.

which kindled the sensibilities of his hearers. His enthusiasm in presenting and defending the Edwardean theology, awakened the sympathy of many in the church, while his tact and culture enlisted friends in the congregation. He was a good organizer, and had much tact in dealing with men. The affairs of the church, which had fallen into neglect, were straightened and reduced to order; discipline was restored, and the spiritual forces of the gospel soon began to assert their power in the community. Worldly men were troubled, and various methods were tried to hinder the growing seriousness. The opposition to his preaching, however, served to unite the hearts of his supporters,* and begat in them a watchful and earnest spirit. Men of prominence for ability and influence were brought into the church, and a new tone of spiritual activity animated the whole body. As the opposition to his ministry turned on questions of theological belief,† an earnest controversy arose, in which the doctrinal position of the majority was clearly defined. No wisdom or prudence, on the part of the pastor, could prevent the open rupture which resulted in a secession of part of the church and congregation. "The year 1824," writes the Rev. Silas Aiken, "brought with it severe trials to both the pastor and the church, in the withdrawment of several members, in order to form a Unitarian church in connection with a new society‡ recently established, and to come under the pastoral care of Rev. E. Q. Sewall. But in all these trials the Lord assisted them. He brought Zion

* The Tuesday afternoon prayer-meeting, which is still maintained by the church, was instituted at the house of the junior pastor during these trials, April 4, 1823.

† The style and matter of the discussion that agitated this community, may be learned by consulting the files of the Farmer's Cabinet for 1817-18.

‡ At a special town-meeting, Nov. 18th, 1822, the disaffected members of Mr. Lord's congregation asked the use of the church their proportion of the time; vote,—yeas, 87, nays, 131. 1824, March 27, Charles H. Atherton, David Holmes, Ephraim Blanchard, Elisha F. Wallace, and their associates, formed themselves into a religious society, and took the name and style of "The Christian Society in Amherst." The Unitarian meeting-house (63x45 feet) was raised June 9, 1835, under direction of John Crombie, Jr., of New Boston. Dedicated, Nov. 24. Sermon by Rev. Mr. Maynard, pastor, from Acts 17:24. This house is now occupied by the Baptists.

out of all her troubles, and set her feet in a large place." On the failure of his voice, Mr. Lord resigned, and, having a call to the presidency of Dartmouth college, he was dismissed Nov. 22, 1828, to accept that office.* The additions to the church under his ministry gave new force to the institutions of religion; the church was homogeneous in sentiment, its discipline reëstablished, and the way prepared for the enlargement of its numbers on the evangelical basis.

On the 4th March of the following year, in compliance with a unanimous call from the Congregational church and society (the relation of the town to the support of the ministry having ceased), Rev. Silas Aiken was settled. The services of his ordination † are still remembered, and the esteemed pastors who officiated at the time. Mr. Aiken brought to the ministry certain gifts by which he was qualified for special usefulness in this field. He had not the polished manners and graceful address of Dr. Lord. He was tall and strongly built, with a certain abruptness and angularity of movement consequent upon a shy and reserved nature. He had vigorous health, strong lungs, a stalwart frame, great natural shrewdness, and a masculine understanding. He analyzed his subject and laid out the plan with strong handling, and the filling up was wrought with intense feeling. In this was the secret of his power. Often, when preaching, the emotions of his great heart hurried him on into strains

---

* 1828. Dec. 16th, Perley Raymond, Timothy D. Wood, and John Hazeltine, with their associates, united in forming a religious society by the name of the "First Methodist Society in Amherst," with the intention of maintaining worship on Chestnut hills. April 9, 1839, at the suggestion of Rev. John Adams, John Haseltine, Solomon Barron, Loammi Eaton, Levi Duncklee, and their associates, formed themselves into a society, taking the name of the "First Methodist Society." In April, 1840, they took possession of the lot, on which their house of worship now stands, and in which slips were sold to members in February, 1841.

† The sermon was preached by Rev. Samuel Green, of Boston; prayer of ordination by Rev. Eli Smith, of Hollis; charge to the pastor by Rev. Dr. Church; fellowship of the churches by Rev. A. Richards; address to the people by Rev. Mr. Nott, of Nashua. Dr. Aiken, son of Phineas Aiken, was born in Bedford, May 14, 1799; graduated at Dartmouth college, 1825; ordained pastor, 1829,—at Amherst till 1837; Park street, Boston, 1837-1848; Rutland, Vt., 1849-1863; trustee Dartmouth college, 1840-1862; died at Rutland, April 7, 1869.

of fervid and subduing eloquence. In these seasons of impassioned address, he literally besought men with tears to be reconciled to God. The success of his ministry in gathering converts was great* beyond precedent. Of the ministry of his successors, Rev. F. A. Adams, PH. D., and Rev. W. T. Savage, D. D., who were both able and scholarly men, I make no sketch. Each of them performed valuable services here, and in other fields of Christian labor they have won an enviable reputation for talents and fidelity.

The church, which was organized in 1741 by six members, in the simplest form of Congregationalism, out of a population of fourteen families, had increased, under the four pastorates which I have delineated, to a membership of three hundred and eight in a population of sixteen hundred, with two other churches in the township. The average of annual additions for the last ninety-three years is ten ; and the whole number, from the formation of the church to this date, must be nearly eleven hundred and fifty.

But the real usefulness of a church and the ordinances of worship is not to be stated in figures. Who shall estimate the value of the influences emanating from this sanctuary, as they have moulded and enriched the minds and hearts of this people and their descendants! Who can trace the various lines of profitable thought, of virtuous endeavor, and self-denying Christian duty here started! Who shall measure the enlargement of mind, the elevation and refinement of feeling, consequent on the manifestation of the truth from this pulpit! Who will tell us how much of sin has been

* In the spring of 1835 the Spirit "came down like showers that water the earth." The week of the annual state Fast was wholly given to the work, with preaching twice a day, inquiry and prayer meetings morning and evening. Business was mainly suspended; and the whole population seemed drawn by a heavenly influence to the house of God. The great question with all seemed to be,—"What must I do to be saved?" Fathers, mothers, children,—in some cases, whole families,—yielded to the Spirit, and became obedient to the heavenly vision. The pastor labored with a strong hand, and willing, joyful heart, characteristically declaring "that though there was much work to be done, when seed-time and harvest came together" it was easy working. As the result of this revival, one hundred and one members united with the church, nearly all of whom honored their professions. [*From the manuscript of Dea. E. D. Boylston.*

restrained, how much of folly prevented, how much of suffering saved, by the counsels here uttered! Who will anticipate the rewards of that consecration which hallowed this territory for more than a century, as it will appear in the divine records of sins forgiven, souls purified, and men redeemed! These servants of Christ, having served their generation by the will of God, have fallen asleep. "They rest from their labors, and their works do follow them."

[At this point, while the speaker paused, the choir sang, with pleasing effect, the following stanzas :

Though earthly shepherds dwell in dust,
The aged and the young;
The watchful eye in darkness closed,
And mute the instructive tongue,—

The eternal Shepherd still survives,
New comfort to impart;
His eye still guides us, and his voice
Still animates our heart.—*Doddrige.*]

The history of church music, as it has been employed in this house and in the earlier sanctuary, would furnish an entertaining chapter. In the absence of any record, as the gift of song runs in families, we may assume that John Seatown, the first deacon of the name and fourth in order of election, was a leader under Pastor Wilkins. We should not probably err in asserting that he pitched the tune and led in the psalm, standing in front and below the pulpit, as his son and successor in office did thirty-five years afterwards. At that period "Sternhold & Hopkins," or the "Bay State Collection of Psalms and Hymns," was used in this vicinity. The choice of tunes did not exceed twelve in the three metres.

One story survives, which deserves preservation for the benefit of distracted parishes. It appears that Pastor Wilkins and the singers had introduced a new hymn book (probably the incoming version of Dr. I. Watts), to which some in the congregation were violently opposed. The excitement was so great that a compromise was attempted by using the new version only for the last tune, "when the opposers retired from the house, rather than hear the words of the devil." "Mr. Wilkins," says the chronicler, "thought these persons did not know what they were opposing." He accordingly arranged an exchange; and the new minister began with the new version, and used it all day. At the last singing the disaffected hearers left the meeting as usual; but when they learned soon after that they had heard the hated tunes all day without knowing it, the opposition became so ludicrous that they were content to say no more about it."

In Mr. Barnard's day "the quiresters" were permitted to sit together; and, while it was their duty to make harmony for others, they did not always maintain peace among themselves. On one occasion, when the singers were in practice for the approaching Fourth of July, some offence was taken; and on the following Sabbath "the chorister, the pastor's son-in-law, found himself alone in the singing-seats. Not willing to sing alone, he also retired. When Mr. Barnard rose in the pulpit, the seats were empty. After the introductory service, he read a hymn. Then, laying down the book with some energy, he called on the congregation to unite in prayer." Not much time elapsed before he took up the singers, "praying that, if they would not unite in praising the Lord in the sanctuary, they might not be permitted to sing together on any occasion whatever. Going on in this strain for some time, the singers thought it best to return. First, the chorister took his place, then the next in rank, until finally, before the close of the prayer, the seats were filled; and the second hymn was responded to with unwonted power." In the closing period of Mr. Barnard's ministry, Jonathan Hildreth acted as chorister, and his services were widely esteemed.

There was a large choir in Dr. Lord's time, as a place in the singing-pews was a coveted distinction; and when the ranks "were full the singing meant something. With bass viol, violin, and brazen instruments (says my informant), and such voices as Benjamin Kendrick's, Ambrose Seaton's, Mary Goss's, and twenty others, male and female, the people could make melody in their hearts if they desired to."

The introduction of organs marks a later period, and brings to mind the assiduous zeal of Mrs. Prentiss, and the almost affectionate solicitude of Bro. Aaron Lawrence, with the sturdy presence, clear tenor voice, and piping violin of Mr. Elbridge Hardy. I could speak of other male and female singers who have contributed to our edification and delight in the sacred service of song and praise.

> "Music, when soft voices die,
> Vibrates in the memory."

I recall the names of many, both of the living and the dead, towards whom we feel more gratitude than we have ever expressed.

The house in which we are assembled occupied the spot on which it was raised, and in substantially the form already described, for 65 years; two generations, with thronging families, had gathered within its capacious walls for worship. Up to the year 1832 the house had been held and controlled by the town, in the interest of the majority. With the change in the statutes, respecting the support of religious institutions in New Hampshire, the town disposed of the house by auction to the highest bidder, reserving only the tower, clock, and bell, when the building became the property of the Congregational society. The necessity of thorough repairs and of improved accommodations for seating the worshippers was manifest to all. The work of remodelling and removing was commenced in 1836, when the building was turned half round, and then moved backwards from the common to the site on which it now stands. The galleries were taken down, the floor raised, new windows inserted, and the building so extended as to embrace the porch which sustained the steeple. By this means a gallery was constructed over the entry, which furnished seats for the choir. With a new pulpit, and pews of the modern pattern, the house was accepted by the congregation from the contractor, Mr. Jona. Knight, with expressions of approbation. The house was reoccupied January 1, 1837, when Dr. Aiken preached a sermon from 2 Chron. 6:18, "on the end for which houses of worship are reared, and the means by which that end can be secured." The occasion was one of memorable interest, as the preacher gave utterance to his earnest thoughts on the duty of public worship, and the obligation that binds men to make the services of the earthly sanctuary the means of preparation for the kingdom of heaven.

From that date no essential changes were made in the structure or furnishing of the house till 1857, when the pulpit was refitted, the aisles recarpeted, and the pews painted, the expense being defrayed by the ladies of the congregation. In 1858 the chapel,* a tasteful and convenient building for social worship was erected by the contributions of individuals. On January 20, 1859, it was dedicated by suitable religious services. Other outlays have been made, as occasions required, for the preservation of the meeting-house and the comfort of the worshippers. By the latest of these appropriations the gallery has been shut off and the audience-room reduced to the original dimensions, the windows furnished with new sash-lights, the close pulpit exchanged for an open platform, with chairs and desk of choice workmanship, while a new and superior organ, on a raised floor, for the singers, at the west side of the pulpit, brings the choir before the audience and within easy communication with the preacher.

It is a pleasant coincidence that, in refurnishing this house, these various improvements,—the organ, the pulpit, furniture, and other valuable accompaniments, the gifts of present and former worshippers, an expression of love to this church and

* The contract for the chapel, taken by Jotham Hartshorn & Sons, was performed in a very satisfactory manner. The entire cost was about $1,300.

of gratitude to God for benefits received here,—should, without special design, have been ready for service to-day.

As the first tones from that noble instrument have called us to

"Praise God, from whom all blessings flow,"

let our hearts respond by a renewed consecration to the author of these mercies,—the God of our salvation.

This house of worship, ante-dating the declaration of the nation's independence, has stood unharmed through the changes of a century. It has survived storms and tempests, the perils of fire, and the fitful vicissitudes of this uncertain climate. It has witnessed the civil revolutions, the modifications of law and executive administrations, which introduced the republican form of government, and have made the United States of America a great name among the nations of the earth. It has also witnessed changes in arts and manufactures, in social customs, employments, modes of travel, and of domestic life, by which we are far removed from the simple,—I might say the straitened,—habits of the fathers.

Of the four generations who have worshipped in this sanctuary, the first two were usually clothed in homespun garments, the handiwork of wives and daughters who put their hands to the distaff, and wrought in wool and flax and divers colors of needle-work. It was no unusual sight, of a Sabbath morning in the olden times, to see at the farmer's door the horse, with saddle and pillion, prepared for the meeting. The older boys and girls having set forth on foot at an earlier hour,—the father mounted to hold a child in front, and the mother taking the seat behind, with the youngest in her arms,—the family became one troop as they reached the place of worship. It seems hardly credible, that, as late as 1820, women of excellent standing in the out-districts walked to meeting with bare feet, carrying shoes and stockings in hand until nearing the church, when they put on these articles for the service, which were to be taken off again as they went home. Amidst the snows of winter, ox-sleds were often in requisition for the accommodation of neighboring households and the abounding delight of the young people. At the close of the religious services by which this house was dedicated, we are told by Dea. Samuel Wilkins that the assembled ministers and dignitaries dined at the house of his father. The principal dish on the table was hasty-pudding and milk. "While they were eating, he told them a ludicrous story about catching a sheep, at which 'ye fathers were well pleased, and the pudding flew well.'"

Other details of that and succeeding periods would have an equally strange and novel air to the larger portion of this audience. The state and customs of society existing in Dr. Lord's day are very much changed. The great progress in the knowledge and science of music, the greatly enlarged and improved collections of psalmody, all the new and perfected arrangements for lighting and warming our houses of worship, illustrate the real advancement which has been made in our civilization. Very few, probably, in this house have heard a hymn "lined off" by the pastor in the Sabbath worship. That practice has ceased with the noise of viols, and the long drawn note of the pitch pipe. The days of the pillion, of foot-stoves, of home-spun garments and the tything-men, are gone—*gone*, as irrecoverably as the stone horse-block from which sheriff Kelley proclaimed, by beat of drum, the birth-day of the nation, on the 18th of July, 1776.

The meeting-house, as the name indicates, was the place of all public gatherings. Here the citizens assembled in their primary meetings to vote on town affairs; here they rallied in patriotic conventions; here they listened on recurring anniversaries to civic orations, agricultural addresses, educational lecturers, and whatever might be judged profitable to the body politic. Jury trials have, on more than one occasion, been held within these walls, and, in 1794, the members of the two houses of the New Hampshire legislature stood here, with uncovered heads, to unite in seeking the Divine guidance and blessing on their deliberations. It is probable that the sessions of the larger branch of that body were held in this room, for the want of better accommodations.

This house, always open to the sons and daughters of sorsow, has not been frequently used for funeral services,—our afflicted families preferring a more private ceremonial; and it has never been a fashion with us to resort to this place for the solemnization of marriages. Yet no other spot is associated more vividly with all those social changes—the seasons of sorrow and of joy that make life memorable—than this sanctuary. Hither you came in early childhood, delighting in the stirs and shows of the goodly company that thronged the way to the place of worship. Here you felt that mysterious pressure of reverent sentiment that accompanies the presence of large numbers really intent on God's worship. Here you listened to prayer and praise, with emotions intensified by conscious union with others engaged in the same duty. Here you have been pleased and wearied,—sometimes longing to hear more, and then impatient to be released, as your mood or your tastes may have harmonized with the preacher's efforts. Here, too, you have known the power of revealed truth, enlightening your conscience, searching your understanding, and awakening a sense of accountability unfelt elsewhere. Whatever your use or improvement of the hours spent here, I know there are associations connected with the old meeting-house that stir the deepest springs of your being. There is something in the company of fathers and mothers, of kindred, companions, and neighbors, which lends a pathos and weight to the word spoken here that few can resist. The audience-room may be architecturally defective, the walls cold and unsightly; there may be much that is grotesque in the dress or conduct of the worshippers; and yet, if Christ be preached and God worshipped, the rude structure is thereby sanctified, and we say, This is holy ground.

This is true of hundreds of our New England temples, but emphatically is it true to us, when we stand in the sanctuary where our fathers worshipped; when we crowd the pews where mothers, sisters, and brothers sat by our sides and heard the gospel; when we walk the aisles where we took upon us the vows of the Christian profession, "avouching the Lord to be our God, and giving ourselves to Jesus Christ as the only Saviour." Here we "were made partakers of the heavenly gift, and tasted the powers of the world to come."

"But will God in very deed dwell with men upon earth?" Of a truth, "the Lord our God hath been with us, as He was with our fathers," and "the glory of this latter house has been greater than of the former." Whatever the recognized value of the established institutions of religion, in their bearings on the cause of good order, sound morals, and popular education; however important the meeting-house, as a source of healthful social influences, upholding law, encouraging virtue, and strengthening all humane and philanthropic sentiments,—still, its supremest power comes of the vital forces of the gospel, when the preaching of Jesus Christ and him crucified becomes the wisdom and the power of God unto salvation. Very memorable have been the displays of Divine grace in this sanctuary. In the great ingatherings of 1831 and 1835, in 1842, and again in 1849, this church received large accessions to its numbers and strength. Multitudes thronged these seats during those seasons of religious impression, and the consequent changes in character and conduct attest the genuineness of the work. The ways of the Spirit are by no means uniform, but, whenever He visits our congregations, the word becomes quick and powerful, a revealer of the thoughts and intents of the heart. Then sinners are convinced of sin and acknowledge their errors: then they see the attractions of the cross, and give themselves to the service of Christ, the great Redeemer. In the experience of this renewing, sanctifying power of the truth, men attest the superiority of the gospel to all other instrumentalities for reforming the guilty, and delivering the enslaved from the bondage of sin. Hence, the causes of temperance, of missions, and of moral reformations find their strength in the sanctuary. Here are witnessed revivals of the spirit of missions, renewed consecrations to the work of temperance and benevolence. As an illustration of this last experience, let me quote what is recorded of such a revival at the meeting of the General Association in this house in 1832: "On Wednesday, at the anniversary of the New Hampshire Bible Society, so enlarged were the hearts of the people of God, that a contribution was taken up of $205.85, and a subscription made amounting to $819.50, besides two gold necklaces worth $20. But on Thursday, at the close of the missionary sermon by Rev. Edward L. Parker, of Derry, a missionary spirit broke out and pervaded the great congregation, and such a scene was opened as never before was witnessed in New Hampshire." It was resolved to raise the ensuing year $6,000 for the New Hampshire Missionary Society, a large portion of which was pledged on the spot. About one hundred and twenty entered their names as life members. The collection, including money and jewelry, was liberal beyond the expectation of the largest hearts. Old Testament times seemed to have returned, when "they came, both men and women, as many as were willing hearted, and brought bracelets, and ear-rings, and rings, and tablets, all jewels of gold: and every man that offered, offered an offering of gold unto the Lord."*

With such testimonies of the Divine influence, opening the heart and transforming the will, might be connected the relation of personal experiences by which the lives of many have been lifted to a superior plane, and the world made better by their example. Very gladly would I follow the history and recount the deeds of some of the early members of this church. I should be glad to unfold the part they took in the

---

* **Dr. Bouton's Historical Discourse at Boscawen, 1859, p. 45.**

councils of the town, and the self-denial they exhibited in planting and sustaining the institutions by which we have so largely profited. In the study of their principles and conduct, we might learn the sources of that far-seeing wisdom and that persistent courage which wrested victories out of defeat, and enabled them, in the conflict of opinions, to adopt that line of practical administration which grants liberty without licentiousness, and maintains law without oppression. Among the acts, resolves, and other papers submitted to the town and determining its action in the forming period of our history, from 1763 to 1789, there are many sentiments which command our admiration for their just expression of moral and political truth. After a survey of the lives of the men who occupied leading positions in the church and community,—whose sepulchres are with us unto this day,—it would not be less profitable to follow the steps and trace the influence of many who have gone forth from this church to find employment elsewhere. I would gladly repeat the record of some who have finished their course, having kept the faith. I can think of one, and another, and another, of godly men and saintly women, who, having witnessed a good confession in larger spheres, have chosen to rest at last in our village cemetery. Their memory is blessed. I have in mind others, yet active, who are pillars of beauty and strength in the towns and cities of their adoption, who remember with liveliest gratitude the old meeting-house, where in early childhood they were taught the sure principles of the word of God, and where, in opening manhood, they entered into covenant with Christ and his people. Other witnesses there are, daughters like unto corner stones, polished after the similitude of a palace;—but I will not multiply testimonies to prove that the Lord has been with us as he was with the fathers, and that the old meeting-house is not past useful service.

"Peace be within this sacred place,
And joy a constant guest!
With holy gifts and heavenly grace
Be her attendants blest!"

Among the thoughts suggested by this hurried survey of the past and its customs, the habits, usages, and places of worship, the men and women into whose labors we have entered, I mark the unity, the identity of human interests, in all this diversity. How like us in hopes and fears, in anxieties, affections, and joys, the departed generations! How akin in sorrows, sickness, bereavements, and death! We smile perhaps at their errors, pronounce upon their faults, and think that we are better than they. We read of their hardships, their patient endurance, their courageous industry, their reverence for God, their pious observance of the Sabbath, with a conviction that they were better than we. So the balance of our judgment vibrates;—but how like us, in their deepest wants, their aspirations, their hearts' desires! and how clear that the only abiding satisfaction, for us as for them, is in the faithful discharge of duty, the exercise of right affections, and the sustaining power of a hope in the Divine mercy! There is no better lesson accompanying their history than this testimony, that our sufficiency is not of ourselves. Our obligations to the fathers are great. For us they cleared the forests, made highways, reared the churches, wrought out problems in civil and religious polity. We live in better houses, have more freedom, more wealth, more culture and privileges, because of their labors; but in all that experience, so varied and instructive, comes the repeated admonition,—"Man shall not live by bread alone!"

Again: as we go over the history, it occurs to us that all these persons, whatever their occupations or characters, are gone! They have died. Not the chief actors only,—the preachers and singers, the magistrates and deacons, the land-owners, the lawyers and eloquent orators,—but all, the mothers, the maidens, the Monson folks, the federalists, the republicans, the few colored people—all that busy, plotting, striving multitude, those who did and those who did not go to meeting, are dead! And of all that thought, labor, desire, enjoyment, what abides? "The fathers, where are they? and the prophets, do they live forever?" Before another period like this which we review is passed, all of this audience will have joined the mighty congregation of the dead. These dwellers on the western heights, these children from abroad, these citizens from adjoining towns, these familiar faces of neighbors and companions who greet us on the street, will be gone! Some will try to keep alive our names. Some, possibly, may be curious to learn what part we acted, to what end we lived. Whatever the judgment posterity may pronounce on us, let us not forget the final trial that is to search every man's work of what sort it is.

To this end, let us pray,—"The Lord our God be with us as he was with our fathers," enabling us to avoid their errors, to imitate their excellence, and make sure of His salvation.

HISTORY OF THE BAPTIST CHURCH.

BY REV. ALBERT HEALD, PASTOR.

On the second day of the present month (January, 1874), the Baptist church had been constituted forty-four and a half years. Prior to its formation there were a number of persons, living in various parts of the town, who held the distinctive sentiments of the Baptists; but these resided chiefly on Chestnut hill and in that vicinity. Many of these held their relations with different churches in neighboring towns; others had not connected themselves with any religious body.

The first organization for the purpose of securing preaching was formed October 6, 1828, with the following declaration of purpose: "Being deeply sensible of the importance of the *preached* as well as the *written word*, to ourselves and families; the privations that we, who live in this vicinity, have to undergo, by being located so far from the ministrations; and believing that it is our duty to contribute to the support of a preached gospel, and that united exertions are both desirable and beneficial,—we feel it our duty and privilege to procure as many persons in this region as are willing to sign this paper for the purpose of forming a religious society, denominated the First Baptist Society, in Amherst, N. H."

To this the following names were subscribed at its formation, to which many others were afterwards added:

Ralph Holbrook,	James Prince,
Ebenezer Holbrook,	Robert Fletcher,
Oliver Mears,	Otis Fletcher,
Franklin Mears,	Benjamin Damon,
Henry Tewksbury,	John Washer,
Joseph Harvill,	Benjamin R. Shepherd,
John Rollins,	Joseph Harriden.

A constitution was prepared and adopted, in which two very important principles are announced as the fundamental ground of their action:

"1. That morality and piety, governed on evangelical principles, give the best and greatest happiness in society.

"2. That the public worship of the Deity is the best way of promoting this morality and piety."

The church was organized on July 2, 1829. Letters were sent to the churches in Londonderry, Milford, New Boston, Weare, and Goffstown.

The following ministers were present: Rev. Samuel Abbott and Rev. Isaac Durrah, Londonderry; Rev. Samuel Everet, Milford; Rev. John Atwood, New Boston; and Rev. Simon Fletcher, Goffstown.

The council consisted of twelve members. Rev. Samuel Abbott was chosen moderator, and Rev. S. Fletcher, clerk.

There is no record of the original members of the church. A few may be still living, but they have long since removed their relation to other churches, or gone to their rest and reward.

They held their meetings at first on Chestnut hill, and continued them there until 1837.

In 1835, on February 3, a protracted meeting was commenced, conducted by Rev. John Peacock, and continued sixteen days. This was the commencement of one of the most extensive revivals ever enjoyed in this community. The first sermon was preached, by the leader of the meeting, from John 11:56,—"What think ye, that he will not come up to the feast?" He did come in wonderful power, so that, literally, there was not room enough to receive the blessing. Multitudes came from all the surrounding sections, were filled, and carried away the sweet influence of the Spirit's presence. The work spread to the north, east, south, and west. The school-house where they held their meetings became altogether too strait for them. The windows were removed from the north end of the house, and large numbers were accommodated on the ground or ledge that rose gradually from the north side of the building. That they could have been comfortable at this season was remarkable. He who moved in the meeting, melting hard hearts, ordered the weather so that it met their circumstances. Another method was also adopted to meet the emergency: the congregation was divided. In the morning, during a part of the time, the unconverted assembled at the school-house, while Christians met at the house of Dea. J. Harvill,—the former to listen to a sermon, and the latter to hold a season of prayer. In the afternoon the order was reversed. Christians met at the school-house, and anxious inquirers at the private dwelling. There are many now living who remember these scenes very distinctly, and are cheered as they recount what God did for them.

Rev. J. Peacock, who was a native of Amherst, and led these meetings, after nearly forty years of hard service, with glorious results, as an evangelist, has returned to his native town, expecting to make it his home the remainder of his days, and rest at last with his kindred. He was greatly assisted in these meetings by Rev. Silas Aiken, then pastor of the Congregationalist church, and Rev. Thomas Savage, of Bedford. The church, which has for one hundred years worshipped in this house, received the largest accessions to its numbers during this year of any for the century just now closed. There were many scores that found Christ, either directly or indirectly, from the interest connected with this protracted effort.

On these hills was this church first constituted: and it may be asked why they did not remain there. Paradoxical as it may seem, it was because God had so abundantly blessed them. This church was not very much strengthened, and this was owing mainly to their location. As one result of the revival, they dismissed a part of their number to form a church at Bedford. Like the family in an out-of-the-way place on the hills, their spiritual children did not remain at home. Yet for a time they clung to the hill, for there were many precious associations clustering around it. They loved the place, for here had God gloriously manifested the power of his grace and truth.

A committee was appointed to procure a lot upon which to build a meeting-house. The place was selected and staked out; but this was the extent of the movement in this direction. These Christians had before gone long distances to meeting; and they could again make a sacrifice for the cause. Some of them had made a journey very regularly to Milford, of eighteen miles out and back, to attend meeting on the Sabbath. It must be conceded that something more than mere captiousness, or caprice, or prejudice prompted them, especially when they were obliged to pass this house, where such men as Rev. Nathan Lord and Rev. Silas Aiken preached the gospel with so much earnestness and power.

In 1837 they moved their meeting to the village. To many of them it was a great sacrifice. For a time they had no certain abiding-place. Sometimes they worshipped in the schoolhouse, sometimes in a hall over a store situated on the common near where the monument now stands, and sometimes in the court-house. Nov. 19th, 1841, the record reads,—"Being deprived of the use of the court-house, we made arrangement to worship in the Unitarian house." This they continued to do for a part of the time for three years, when the house was conveyed by the Christian society to the First Baptist society in Amherst, by deed dated April 7, 1844.

A condition in the subscription to the shares for the building of this house was, that the Christian society should transfer the house to any other religious society when they should hold two thirds of the pews in the same. This condition being secured to the Baptist society by purchase and transfer, at an expense of between $1,000 and $1,100, it was accordingly deeded to them by said Christian society, and it has for the last thirty years been their place of worship. In 1851 the house was repaired at an expense of $300, and again, in 1870, at an expense of $500.

BEQUESTS. The first bequest was made by Fanny G. Flinn, May 8th, 1838, of $90, to be expended in annual instalments of $5 each. The second was made by James Prince, of the income of $200 for ten years. The third was left by Joseph Harvill, of $200. The fourth, of $1,000, by Mrs. Lucy Coggin, to purchase a parsonage, was offered on condition that the church and society would raise $500 to repair the meeting-house;—which was done. Mr. Luther Coggin gave the lumber to build a stable. Miss S. L. Lawrence left by will $250 to purchase a bell. This now amounts to about $300. Besides these, there have been gifts of a Bible and hymn-book for the desk, a cabinet organ for the choir, chairs for the altar, and a beautiful communion set, by Mrs. Mary Twiss and her children.

PASTORS. The church was supplied by different individuals, for a short period each, for the first twelve years:

Rev. MASON BALL—Settled Aug. 1, 1841; closed his labors Feb. 18, 1844.

Rev. AARON HAYES—Settled March 17, 1844; closed his labors March 30, 1845.

Rev. AMASA BROWN—Settled May 2, 1845; closed his labors April 7, 1847.

Rev. DAVID BURROUGHS—Settled Aug. 1, 1849; closed his labors Dec., 1854.

Rev. SAMUEL JONES—Settled May 11, 1856; closed his labors May 10, 1857.

The pulpit was supplied, during the winter of 1857–58, by Rev. JOHN H. THYNG. During the winter of 1858–59 Rev. SAMUEL COOK supplied the church.

Rev. AMOS W. BOARDMAN—Settled July 31, 1859; closed his labors July 14, 1861.

Rev. J. BASKWELL—Settled Dec. 4, 1863; closed his labors Dec. 31, 1865.

Rev. JOHN PEACOCK supplied the church from Feb. 1, 1866, for nearly two years.

Rev. Eli P. Noyes—Settled April 1, 1868; closed his labors Nov. 1, 1870.

Rev. Albert Heald—Settled Jan. 1, 1870, whose pastorate still continues.

Deacons. The church has been served by nine deacons:

1. Benj. Damon,
2. Joseph Harvill,
3. William Goodnow,
4. Simeon Wilson,
5. Edward M. Holt,
6. Joseph Russell,
7. Samuel Fletcher,
8. Josiah M. Parker,
9. Daniel Cram.

Statistics. About three hundred have united with the church. It is impossible to decide correctly from the records. All the original names are wanting. One hundred and ten have been baptized; one hundred and forty added by letter, and ten by experience. Some have been added when no record has been made; and some evidently dismissed in the same manner.

Incidents. The first communion occurred on August 16, 1829; the first baptism, November 7, of the same year. The first case of discipline was commenced January 15, 1832. The case was continued, and April 14th it voted to give Sister N. seven months to become reconciled; quite a probation, but not a hundredth part as long as God grants to many a poor sinner to become reconciled to him. On July 6, 1833, this probation closed without a reconciliation,—the seven months having been lengthened to fifteen.

The first death occurred March 27, 1846, sixteen years and eight months after the organization; the last death, December 27, 1873, of brother Willie P. Upton, who united about eighteen months before. He was an active, growing Christian, and a young man of much promise. May all the members be as well prepared and as willing to go, when their Lord shall call for them, as was this young brother.

A BRIEF HISTORICAL SKETCH

OF THE

CHURCH IN MONT VERNON,

PRESENTED BY THE ACTING PASTOR,

REV. S. H. KEELER, D. D.,

At the Centennial of the Erection of the Congregational Meeting-house, in Amherst, January 18, 1874.

The daughter of ninety-three, residing at Mont Vernon, having been invited by her venerable mother, aged one hundred and thirty-three, to hold a united service with her, January 18, 1874, in observance of the centennial of the erection of her sanctuary, in which they formerly worshipped together, cheerfully complied with the request, gave up her public worship at home, and, with her pastor, passed the Sabbath with the parent church.

Having in the morning listened with great interest to the historical sermon by Rev. Dr. Davis, and having been requested to occupy a part of the afternoon in reminiscences of the church in Mont Vernon, the pastor presented the following brief historical sketch. Having also been requested to furnish a copy of the same, that it might be published with the sermon of Dr. Davis and other services of the day, the following pages, with some additions, are hereby offered for the above purpose:

The church in Mont Vernon was organized as the second church in Amherst, September, 1780, by a council called for that purpose. Who composed the council I have not been able to ascertain, as no records of these transactions are to be found, nor of the church itself, for some thirteen years, nor have I been able to learn the number that composed the church at its formation. There is traditional proof, however, that the original members were quite remarkable for their sound, intelligent orthodoxy, and the quiet yet decided earnestness of their piety. I have been informed, also, that, soon after the organization of the church, the Rev. Mr. Coggin, of Chelmsford, Mass., preached to a large congregation in Major Cole's barn, on the importance of erecting, without delay, a house of worship; an undertaking of no small difficulty, amid the pecuniary stress of those revolutionary days. The sermon, however, was decidedly effective. On the following April, each farmer in the settlement not only contributed freely his quota of timber, which, according to the fashion of those times, was *timber with a witness*, both in *dimensions and weight*, but they drew it quite the last of the month, on a depth of ice-crusted snow, above which neither fence nor wall was visible. Fifty-four persons were legally constituted the Second Parish in Amherst, in June, 1781.

They are spoken of as a band of resolute, noble, and pious men, whose orthodoxy was unquestionable, and who felt that they were laying the foundation for future generations. A lot of land having been given to the parish by Lieut. James Woodbury, the house was erected with as little delay as possible, and gradually finished, as the people were able. There is no record of its formal dedication. During the first winter, so urgent was the demand for the church, that, though but partially fitted up for the purpose, and entirely destitute of any warming apparatus, yet the house was well filled with worshippers, some of whom walked even from Chestnut hills, five miles distant. Among these were not only strong men, but noble and resolute women.

The new church and parish, although supplied with preaching by several candidates for the pastorate, were destitute of a settled minister till Nov. 3, 1785, when Rev. John Bruce became their first pastor. He was a native of Marlboro', Mass., born Aug. 31, 1757; a graduate of Dartmouth college at the age of twenty-four, where, by his studious habits, his mild, serious, and dutiful character, he won from his teachers the title of "good Mr. Bruce." After a pastorate of some twenty-five years,—the longest of any of his successors,—he suddenly died of apoplexy, aged fifty-one, on the Sabbath morning of March 12, 1809, with his armor on. While his people had assembled and were waiting for their pastor, a messenger announced the sad intelligence of his death,—an event sorrowful to them, but joyful to him. His ministry was eminently successful. The whole number added to the church during his pastorate cannot be definitely stated, as for several years its records are not to be found. A memorandum, however, in the hand-writing of Mr. Bruce, has been found, containing evidently a list of church members prior to 1799, making the membership up to that time, by letter and by profession, one hundred and ten. The year 1799 was rendered memorable not only by the first religious revival enjoyed by this church, but as the first ever known in this region. The blessed result of it to this church was the addition of fifty members by profession, making the whole number added during Mr. Bruce's ministry one hundred and sixty. The happy influence of this revival was not limited to this church, but extended far and wide among neighboring churches. Many years afterwards, Rev. Mr. Bradford, of Francestown, said that, when informed of the numbers converted to Christ in Mont Vernon, he was so much affected that he shut himself up for the day, and wept and prayed. This revival was not only the harbinger, but the glorious beginning, of no less than six or seven seasons of special religious interest with which the church has been favored since that period.

The next pastor of this church was Rev. Stephen Chapin, a graduate of Harvard, and a pupil of Dr. Emmons. He was installed November, 1809, and, after an efficient pastorate of nine years, was dismissed November 18, 1818. During his ministry, one hundred and fifteen were added to the church. As the result of a revival in 1817, fifty-one professed Christ on one occasion. The cause of his dismission was a change of views in regard to the mode and subjects of baptism. He afterwards received the honorary title of D. D., and died while president of Columbia college, Washington, D. C., October 1, 1846, aged 67. The next pastor of the church was Rev. Ebenezer Cheever, a graduate of Bowdoin college. He was ordained December 18, 1819, and, after a pastorate of between three and four years, was dismissed April 8, 1823. Twenty-two members were added to the church during his ministry. During the same period, in 1820, the *first Sabbath-school* of the church and society was organized.

It was composed of *children only.* During his ministry, thirty-nine children were consecrated to God by baptism.

Mr. Cheever was succeeded by Rev. Nathaniel Kingsbury, who was ordained November 8, 1823, and, after a ministry of between twelve and thirteen years, was dismissed, on account of ill health, April 6, 1836. His pastorate was one of the most prosperous and successful of those enjoyed by the church. It was blessed by two revivals of great power and thrilling interest,—one in 1828, resulting in an addition of thirty-four to the church, the other in 1831,—that period of protracted meetings and of remarkable revival scenes, the result of which was an addition to the church of some sixty by profession. Prayer-meetings, held at sunrise, were sustained for months, and converts went forth into remote districts to aid in social meetings, even during the busiest seasons of the year. And yet, so did God favor his people with health, with sunshine and showers, that their *temporal* prosperity, even, was never greater. The whole number of members received to the church by letter and profession, during the ministry of Mr. Kingsbury, was one hundred and fifty-four. This period was distinguished also as the beginning of the temperance reform in Mont Vernon. The difficulties which had to be met at that day can hardly be imagined now. Then public opinion was so opposed to it, that even church members would indignantly leave the sanctuary if the subject was alluded to in the pulpit. And it is said that, as Mr. Kingsbury was passing in the direction of the new road that was being made between Mont Vernon and Milford, he overtook one of his deacons, with two pails of liquor, who advised his minister to go the old road, as the workmen were so intoxicated on the new one that he would be insulted. Through the persevering efforts of pastor and people, however, the tide of intemperance was rolled back, if not entirely stayed, and temperance took its appropriate place in the church from that day. In 1837 the sanctuary was removed to its present location, remodelled, and furnished with a bell and organ; it was also supplied with furnaces, and otherwise rendered commodious and comfortable.

The next settled pastor was Rev. Edwin Jennison, a graduate from the Theological Seminary at Andover. He was installed

April 6, 1836, and, after a ministry of a little more than five years, was dismissed on account of ill health, Aug. 19, 1841. He was regarded as a superior sermonizer, but seldom visited his people. Twenty-three were added to the church during his ministry. His health continuing to fail, he visited Europe, and was afterwards settled at Ashburnham, Mass. Rev. Mr. Jennison was succeeded by Rev. B. Smith, a graduate of Dartmouth. He was installed April 19, 1841, and, after a ministry of some nine years, was dismissed April 30, 1850. During his pastorate, thirty-two were added to the church. Several important cases of discipline were settled; and strong ground was taken by the church against slavery and slaveholders.

His ministry was succeeded by that of Rev. Charles D. Herbert, who was installed Nov. 6, 1850. After a pastorate of between five and six years, he was dismissed July 21, 1856. During this period, fifty-five were added to the church. In 1852, quite a number in the academy became hopefully the disciples of Christ. The church then numbered one hundred and sixty-three, and the average age of the members was about fifty-six years.

The pastorate of Rev. Mr. Herbert was followed by that of Rev. Charles E. Lord, a graduate of Dartmouth. He was installed Feb., 1857. After the lapse of some four years, he was dismissed, on account of his wife's ill health, March, 1861. During his ministry, thirteen were added to the church. In a letter of commendation, written to Mr. Lord by a committee of the church chosen for the purpose, after speaking of their regret at parting with him, and of the growing attachment of the church and people to him, the committee bear the following testimony to his ministrations: "They have been highly acceptable, and his preaching clear and instructive; and no difficulties have occurred to mar the enjoyment of the retrospect."

The ministry of Mr. Lord was followed by that of Rev. Geo. E. Sanborn, a graduate of Amherst college, Mass. He was installed April 2, 1862, and, after a pastorate of three years, was dismissed May 29, 1865, to accept a call from Northboro', Mass. Nine were received to the church during his ministry. The church records bear the following testimony of the regard of the church for Mr. Sanborn while their pastor: "*Resolved*,

That this church highly appreciate his ministerial and pastoral labors, and greatly regret that the ties which have bound him and them together should be so soon sundered; and they consent to it only at the call of duty."

As successor to Mr. Sanborn, the Rev. B. M. Frink was installed over this church and people Nov. 1, 1865, and was dismissed to accept a call from the Central church, Portland, Me., Oct. 23, 1867. During his pastorate of some two years, forty-seven were added to the church. A majority of these were received as the fruits of a revival of religion which occurred during the winter and spring of 1866,—a period of great and general interest, the results of which were precious. The ministry of Mr. Frink was eminently active, acceptable, and laborious. Added to the good results already noticed, it should be mentioned that the pulpit was appropriately remodelled and rendered more convenient and attractive, and the present commodious and much needed parsonage was erected. Both these improvements were largely owing to his personal and persevering efforts, aided by the liberal offerings of the church and people.

The present acting pastor of the church and people was a graduate of Middlebury college, Vt., and, also, of the Theological Seminary, Andover, Mass. He commenced his stated ministry in Mont Vernon April 1, 1868, having supplied the pulpit for several Sabbaths the previous winter. He declined the request of the church and people for his installation, because, when he began his labors among them, he thought his ministry might be so brief that it might not be best either for him or them. Had he supposed that his pastorate would be as protracted and pleasant as it has been, he would not only have yielded to the request of the church and people for installation, but acted upon his own conviction, as a general principle, that a regularly settled pastor is always preferable, other things being equal, to the comparatively unsettled relation of an acting pastor. For nearly six years the present ministry has been one of great harmony and pleasure, and attended with most unexpected success, on the part of the incumbent. Seconded by the willing coöperation of the church and people, a debt owed by the latter, of some six hundred dollars, has been cancelled, the parsonage has been improved, the sanctuary has been rendered more commodious and attractive, the organ has been replaced by one better suited to the service of sacred song; and the large expense of these and other improvements has been cheerfully met. It should be mentioned, also, that in so doing the church and parish have been essentially aided by the Female Home Circle, who, in various ways, have raised some fourteen hundred dollars. During the present pastorate, some eighty have been added to the church, making an aggregate of some fifteen per year. Of this number, fifty-three have been added during the year 1873. Most of these are the precious fruit of the revival of religion which occurred in connection with a series of religious meetings held with the church and people the last of April, the pastor being aided by Rev. Mr. Potter, the evangelist. The religious interest thus begun continued through the summer and autumn, and, though lessened in degree, still continues.

One of the most interesting and even remarkable results of this revival is, that the large majority of those who have expressed hope in Christ, and united with the church, are in the meridian of life, men of influence, and eight or ten husbands and their wives; there were also several youth, and one man past four score years. By these additions the things that remained have been strengthened, and the prosperity and perpetuity of the church, which had been seriously endangered by deaths and removals, have been promoted. The whole number who have united with the church since its formation in 1780 is not far from eight hundred. And, notwithstanding the changes by which it has been diminished since then, its present number is not far from one hundred and seventy, resident and non-resident. The church has sent forth *eight ministers*,—two at a very early day, viz., Joshua Howard and Daniel Weston; more recently, Solomon Kittredge, Charles B. Kittredge, J. W. Perkins, Darwin Adams, H. A. Kendall, and J. C. Bryant. It has also supplied the churches in the cities and large towns with some of their most efficient members. It is estimated that some fifty young men belonging to Mont Vernon have been prepared for usefulness, and gone forth to exert it elsewhere, within the last fifteen years, and perhaps as many young women; and, although it is gratifying to know that they are benefiting other communities and other churches, it has been evidently at the expense of this church and people; and the more favored churches and parishes are verily their debtors. And the same is true, doubtless, with reference to very many of our rural places in the State.

Such is a brief and imperfect review of the church and parish of Mont Vernon, from 1780 to 1874, a period of nearly ninety-four years. The compiler has gathered the facts and events with which it is fraught from the most reliable sources within his reach,—partly from the history of the churches of New Hampshire, and partly from the church records of more recent date. It is obviously suggestive of interesting and instructive lessons, honorable to God, and pertinent to the present generation. It obviously teaches the hopeful and encouraging fact, that though pastors may pass away, and many who once composed the church may not continue, by reason of death and other removals, yet the church itself lives, and will be immortal till its mission is fulfilled. What a lesson of gratitude does the contrast between the privations of the fathers and mothers of the past, and the privileges of to-day, read to the present generation! and how does it enhance their obligation! How manifest, moreover, the faithfulness of God to his gracious promise,—"Them that honor me I will honor."

REMINISCENCES

OF

FORMER CITIZENS AND NATIVES OF AMHERST.

BY DANIEL F. SECOMB, CONCORD, N. H.

One hundred years ago our fathers met to dedicate the house their hands had built to the worship of the Builder of the Universe. To-day, but one person then living is numbered among the living inhabitants of our town. Scattered far and near, the ashes of the congregation then assembled rest in peace. Their work is done. What remains of it is with us. We may profit by their labors, and imitate their virtues.

The long contest for the possession of the North American continent, between France and her savage allies on one hand, and Great Britain and her colonies on the other, had been closed a few years before by the capture of Quebec, and the subsequent cession of the French colonies to the English, when the English government, finding itself heavily in debt, proposed to increase its revenue by taxing its thriving colonies. Before conceding this claim, the colonists asked for a representation in parliament, contending that taxation and representation should go together. This being denied, a conflict between the parties became inevitable. The sturdy backwoodsmen, descendants of English Puritans and Scotch Presbyterians, who had fought and conquered savages and wild beasts, met in deadly combat the trained soldiers of the mother land.

With all its serious aspects, the contest had in it a good deal of a grim sort of humor. When the tea was forced upon the Bostonians, it was received under protest; but a teapot of generous dimensions was soon found by his Majesty's loyal subjects to steep it in, the finny inhabitants of Boston harbor being afforded an opportunity to participate in the drinking. And when the demand was made upon the colonists to deliver up their arms, the Spartan answer—"Come and take them"—was soon understood to include what might be found with them. Our fathers entered into the discussions of those stormy times with spirit. One month before the dedication of the house, the tea-party had been given at Boston; and fifteen months later came the opening conflicts of the war at Lexington common and Concord bridge.

In May, 1775, says Mr. Fox, in the history of Dunstable, the county of Hillsborough, with a population of fifteen thousand nine hundred and forty-eight, had six hundred and fifty men in the army, or a little more than one to every twenty-five of its inhabitants; and its shire town was certainly not behind its neighbors in patriotism.

In April, 1776, two hundred and one of its male citizens above twenty-one years of age signed a paper, now on file in the office of the secretary of state, pledging themselves, "to the utmost of their power, at the risk of their lives and fortunes, with arms, to oppose the hostile proceedings of the British fleets and armies against the united American colonies."

Standing first on the list of signers to this bold defiance of British power we find the name of Nahum Baldwin, the village blacksmith, representative to the general court in 1775 and 1780, moderator of the annual town-meeting, town clerk, and selectman in 1778, and for fourteen years a deacon of the church. He was appointed colonel of a regiment, raised in 1776, to reinforce the army in northern New York. This regiment was dismissed at North Castle near the close of the year. This seems to have been the only military commission held by him. He died May 7, 1788, at the age of fifty-three years. Some of his descendants now reside in Antrim, N. H.

Second on the list we find the name of Moses Nichols, a physician of good repute, a native of Reading, Mass., who came to Amherst early in life, and commenced the practice of his profession. In 1765, 1768, and 1773 he served as one of the selectmen, was town clerk in 1773, moderator in 1767, 1769, 1770, 1771, 1773, and 1777, and representative in 1775, 1776, and 1781. He was also register of deeds for Hillsborough county from 1776 until his death. He was appointed colonel of the fifth regiment of militia December 5, 1776, in place of Col. Lutwyche, who had joined the British; commanded the right wing of Stark's army in the battle with the Hessians and tories, near Bennington, August 16, 1777; was colonel of a regiment in General Whipple's brigade, at Rhode Island, in 1778; and, after the close of the war, was appointed brigadier general of the fourth brigade N. H. militia. He died May 23, 1790, aged 49 years.

Stephen Peabody, another signer of the test paper, was an active whig. He was son of William Peabody, who came from Boxford, Mass., to Souhegan West, as early as 1742. He served as one of the selectmen in 1770, 1772, 1773, 1776, and 1779, and was representative in 1779. He was adjutant of Col. Reed's regiment in 1775; major of a regiment, raised for the defence of Portsmouth and its harbor, in 1776; captain of a company, raised for the relief of Ticonderoga, in 1777; aid to Gen. Stark at Bennington; and lieut. colonel, commanding a regiment in

Gen. Whipple's brigade, in 1778. He closed his career September 19, 1782, at the age of thirty-seven. His remains rest in the cemetery at Mont Vernon.

Prior to the first of April, 1777, one hundred and twenty of the citizens of Amherst had been engaged in the war; in this number were two colonels, one major, and five captains. Twenty of its soldiers lost their lives in the course of the war.

In the census of 1840 the following soldiers of the revolution were returned as living in Amherst, Mont Vernon, and Milford:

IN AMHERST.			IN MONT VERNON.		
John Purple,	aged	97	Andrew Leavitt,	aged	87
Thomas Melendy,	"	91	Solomon Kittredge,	"	85
Joseph Crosby,	"	87	Jonathan Lamson,	"	84
Nathan Kendall,	"	85	Zephaniah Kittredge,	"	83
David Fisk,	"	83	Israel Farnum,	"	81
Benjamin Damon,	"	78	Daniel Averill,	"	74
Ephraim Goss,	"	74	IN MILFORD.		
			Samuel Lovejoy,	"	84
			Isaac Burpee,	"	84

Joshua Atherton, one of the four citizens who refused to sign the test paper, was, so far as I am able to learn, the only person who was subjected to any open persecution on account of his opinions. He was confined for a short time in the jail at Exeter, and, with his family, suffered other indignities. He submitted patiently, accepting the consequences of adhering to his convictions; and, at the close of the war, was soon reinstated in the confidence of his fellow citizens. He represented the town in the convention which ratified the federal constitution in 1788, and made a speech (almost the only one made on that occasion, which has been preserved) against its adoption. He was afterwards representative, senator, and attorney-general. He died April 3, 1809, aged 71 years.

The declaration of independence was proclaimed "by the beat of drum," by Moses Kelley, sheriff of the county, from the horse-block, in front of the meeting-house, July 18, 1776. An event now transpiring at Philadelphia may be known to us in five minutes afterwards,—such has been the progress made in the mode of transmitting intelligence within ninety-eight years.

Samuel Dana was one of the worthy citizens of Amherst. The commencement of the revolutionary war found him settled in the ministry, at Groton, Mass., but being suspected of favoring the mother country, he was compelled to relinquish his charge, and for some time was without any settled employment; but in 1783 he was admitted to the practice of the law. On the ninth of January, 1789, he was appointed judge of probate for the county of Hillsborough, which office he held for some years. He died April 2, 1798, at the age of fifty-nine years. He was the first master of Benevolent Lodge, No. 7, Free and Accepted Masons, and was buried with masonic honors, an oration being pronounced on the occasion by Timothy Bigelow, Esq., then a resident here.

One who remembered Judge Dana well, said,—"He was one of the most useful men that ever lived in town—ever active and ready to devise and execute plans for the comfort and convenience of its citizens." Some of his descendants have been men of note, and filled important offices in the state. Among them were Chief Justice Samuel Dana Bell, Senator James Bell, Dr. Luther V. Bell, and Samuel N. Bell, recently member of congress.

John Shepard, Jr., was a native of Concord, Mass., and came here at an early age with his father, who built the mills known as the Shepard mills, on the Souhegan river. He served on the board of selectmen eleven years, and was also town clerk eleven years. His record, after the lapse of a century, is as legible as printed matter. He learned to write by making characters with his finger in the dust which settled on the boards in the grist-mill which he tended. For some years he was justice of the county court and justice of the peace. He died at Milford, December 4, 1802, aged seventy.

William Gordon, died May 8, 1802, at the age of thirty-nine years; graduated at Harvard college 1779; was a senator in the legislature, member of congress three years, and attorney-general. He built the house afterwards occupied by Hon. C. H. Atherton, whose sister he married. His son, William Gordon, graduated at Harvard college, 1806; practised law in Charlestown, N. H.; and died in the Asylum for the Insane, at Brattleborough, Vt., January 12, 1871, aged 83 years.

Robert Means, born in Stewartstown, Ireland, August 28, 1742, settled here prior to the revolution, and soon became one of the leading citizens of the town. By his industry and application to business he acquired a large property. He represented the town in the legislature for three years, was for three years a member of the state Senate, and one year one of the governor's council. He died January 24, 1823.

Benjamin Kendrick, born in Newton, Mass., January 30, 1724, settled on what is now the town farm, then in Monson, in 1749, and became a citizen of Amherst on the annexation of a part of Monson to this place, September 13, 1770. He was town clerk of Monson some years, and selectman of Amherst in 1771. His daughter Anna was the wife of Governor Benjamin Pierce, and the mother of General Franklin Pierce, at one time president of the United States. He died Nov. 13, 1812.

Daniel Warner was a native of Ipswich, Mass.; born June 25, 1745. After residing some years in Nashua, then Dunstable, he settled in Amherst, of which he was a useful and influential citizen. He was employed to take the census of Hillsborough county in 1790, 1800, and 1810. Was lieutenant-colonel, commanding 5th regiment N. H. militia, 1796, moderator of the annual town-meeting in 1798, and represented the town eight years in the general court. He died March 20, 1813. His widow survived until March, 1833. His son Daniel died while a member of Harvard college. John, another son, died while in service in the last war with Great Britain.

Jedediah Kilburn Smith, a native of the town, son of Jonathan Smith, who came here from Danvers, Mass., represented the town in the general court in 1803 and 1804; was a member of the tenth congress, councillor for Hillsborough county four years, senator four years, justice of the court of common pleas, and post-master. He died December 17, 1828, aged 59.

Clifton Clagett, son of Wyseman Clagett, attorney-general of the province of New Hampshire, was born at Portsmouth December 3, 1762, settled in the practice of the law at Litchfield in 1787, removed to Amherst in 1811, and died here January 29, 1829. He was a member of the eighth, fifteenth, and sixteenth congresses, represented Amherst in the general court in 1816, was justice of the superior court for a short time, and judge of probate for Hillsborough county.

Charles Humphrey Atherton, son of Joshua Atherton, was born August 14, 1773. For more than forty years he was register of probate for Hillsborough county, a member of the fourteenth congress, represented the town in the general court in 1823, 1838, and 1839, and was for fifty years one of the leading members of the Hillsborough county bar. He died January 8, 1853. His son, Charles Gordon Atherton, an able lawyer, was born July 4, 1804; graduated at Harvard college 1822; settled in the practice of the law at Nashua; was speaker of the house of representatives three years, representative to congress four years, and senator six years. He died while senator, November 15, 1853.

Horace Greeley was probably the most widely known of the sons of Amherst. He was born of good "Scotch-Irish" stock, in the north-east part of the town, near Bedford line, February 3, 1811. Possessing but few of the advantages enjoyed by youth at the present day, by his energy and perseverance he wrought his way up from poverty and obscurity to a commanding position among the journalists of the country and the world. The *Tribune*, with 1,250,000 readers, was a power in the land, and its editor-in-chief well deserved the title given him by a distinguished contemporary—"Our later Franklin." He died November 29, 1872.

Ephraim Putnam Bradford, mentally and physically one of the greatest of the sons of old Amherst, was son of Capt. John Bradford, a soldier of the revolution, who removed after the close of the war to Hancock, and died there at the age of ninety-three, June 27, 1836. The son was born in the north-east part of the present town of Milford, December 27, 1776; graduated at Harvard college in 1803, and was settled over the Presbyterian church at New Boston, February 26, 1806, where he remained until his death, December 14, 1845. With more ambition and industry he might have graced any city pulpit, or filled most acceptably the place so long held by Dr. Lord at Hanover. To him Clark B. Cochrane, in his centennial address at New Boston, applied the words of the patriarch of Uz,—"Unto him men gave ear, and waited and kept silence at his counsel; they waited for him as for the rain, and they opened their mouth wide as for the latter rain." Silas Aiken (good authority here) once wrote of him,—" He was, literally, one of nature's noblemen, of princely person, with a sonorous, commanding voice, exceedingly fluent and accurate in speech, modelled somewhat after Johnson's style, so richly gifted in mind and heart that, with little preparation, he stood among the first preachers in the state.

Mary Manning Barker, daughter of Dea. Ephraim Barker, to whom he was married September 1, 1806, was a most worthy daughter of old Amherst, and a fit companion for such a man. She was born October 9, 1785, and is still living.

Isaac Hill stands at the head of the graduates from the *Cabinet* office. He was born in what is now Somerville, Mass., April 6, 1788; removed with his family to Ashburnham in 1798; came to Amherst at the age of fourteen, making the journey from Ashburnham on horseback, seated behind his employer. Here he remained seven years. On the 18th of April, 1809, he issued the first number of the *New Hampshire Patriot*, at Concord.* This paper he conducted with much ability for twenty years, during a large part of which time it was the acknowledged leader of the republican journals in the state. Towards the close of his life, in connection with his sons, he published *Hills' New Hampshire Patriot*, and the *Farmers' Monthly Visitor*, a paper devoted to the interests of the farmers of New Hampshire—an exceedingly popular and useful publication.

He represented Concord in the legislature in 1826; was senator from District No. 4 four years; for a short time second comptroller of the U. S. treasury; five years U. S. senator; and three years governor of the state. He died at Washington, March 22, 1851.

Luther Roby, a native of the town, son of James Roby, born January 8, 1801, was, like Gov. Hill, a graduate from the *Cabinet* office. He removed to Concord late in the autumn of 1822, and, on the sixth of January, 1823, issued the first number of the *New Hampshire Statesman*, of which he was man-

---

*One who was intimate with Gov. Hill when in Amherst, relates that he met him while on his way to Concord to establish the *Patriot*. To the inquiry, Where are you going? Hill replied,—"I am going to Concord to print the truth; I have printed lies long enough."

ager and proprietor for the first six months of its existence; he, however, disposed of his interest in it before the close of its first year, but continued in the printing and publishing business. In 1832 he established a stereotype foundry, where he manufactured several sets of plates for the Bible, in pearl type, they being the first of the kind made in New England. Other books were stereotyped at his foundry, and several sets of plates manufactured there were sold to publishers in other places; and large numbers of Bibles, Testaments, and other books have been printed from them.

From plates manufactured in his foundry, and others purchased by him, he has printed 153,000 Bibles, of various styles, 248,000 Testaments, 110,000 copies of Watts's Psalms and Hymns, besides 1,000,000 spelling-books, and large numbers of pamphlets. Latterly he has devoted much time to opening and working the granite ledges in the city of his residence. The introduction of Concord granite, as a building material, will add much to the wealth of the city, and furnish hundreds of its citizens with employment.

For nearly thirty years he was an active member of the fire department of Concord, of which he was chief engineer eight years. He was one of the representatives from Concord in 1837 and 1849.

John Farmer was for about a third of his life a resident of Amherst, coming here in 1805 from Chelmsford, where he was born June 12, 1789. At first he served as clerk in a store, which occupation his feeble health finally compelled him to relinquish. He then engaged in teaching, in which profession he excelled. In 1820 he published an historical sketch of Amherst, which was revised and enlarged in 1837. He also commenced the study of medicine with Dr. Spalding, but shortly relinquished it, and removed to Concord in 1821; there formed a business connection with Dr. Samuel Morrill, in which he continued for a short time. After quitting this, he devoted most of his time to antiquarian and historical researches, in which matters he soon became an acknowledged authority. He was one of the founders of the New Hampshire Historical Society, of which he was for fourteen years the corresponding secretary. Ever ready and willing to aid in any good work, according to his strength and ability. He died, honored and lamented, August 13, 1838. His remains lie beside those of his friend, Joseph Low, the first mayor of Concord, on whose family monument a suitable inscription is placed, in memory of the greatest antiquarian of New Hampshire.

Joseph Low was one of what Dr. Bouton styles the "Amherst colony." It consisted of several young men and women, most of them natives of Amherst, who settled in Concord many years ago, being nearly all of the same age. They were much together, aiding and assisting each other. Most of them acquired a competency, and nearly all of them were among the most respected citizens of the place;—they were Francis N. Fisk, William Fisk and wife (Margaret Dodge), William Low and wife (Grace Nichols), Joseph Low, Benjamin Damon and wife (Sophia Nichols), Peter Robinson, and Isaac Hill. All lived to a good old age,—Francis N. Fisk, the oldest, being ninety years and five months old at the time of his death.

William Fisk, son of Dea. William Fisk, was born at Wenham, Mass., April 20, 1755; came to Amherst with his father in 1773; he served on the board of selectmen for twenty-five consecutive years, eighteen of which he was also town clerk; six years he represented the town in the general court; was senator from the seventh district four years, and twice an elector of president and vice-president of the United States, besides holding other important offices. He was for a long time one of the leaders of the old republican party, and was a man of decided ability. He died June 4, 1831.

A history of the Fiske family was published by Albert A. Fiske, Chicago, 1867.

Samuel Bell resided here for some years. His connection with the Hillsborough bank, of which he was president, injured his popularity here, as the vote for governor in 1819 and subsequent years will show; but the people of the state generally had full confidence in him. He was a member of the senate from the seventh district in 1807 and 1808, in both of which years he was its presiding officer; councillor for Hillsborough district one year; justice of the supreme court three years; governor four years; and senator in congress twelve years, being the second senator from New Hampshire who served two full terms in that body. Although he spoke but seldom in the senate, his advice was sought by his colleagues on all matters of importance, and it is said the memorable speech of Mr. Webster, in reply to Col Hayne, January 26, 1830, was made at his suggestion and request. He died at Chester, December 23, 1850, aged eighty years. "Governor Hill once indorsed him as being one of the best of men, and the very best of governors."

Reuben Dimond Mussey, son of Dr. John Mussey, was born in 1780. For some years in early life he resided on the place now or formerly occupied by Mr. Freeman Bills. Some reminiscences of his boyhood may be found in the *Cabinet* of April 1, 1874. He graduated at Dartmouth college in 1803; studied medicine, and commenced the practice of his profession at Salem, Mass., about 1809, where he remained until 1814, when he accepted a professorship at Hanover, and removed there, remaining until 1838, when he removed to Cincinnati, and became professor of surgery in the Ohio Medical college. This position he filled until 1852, when he became connected with the Miami Medical college as professor of surgery. Leaving this in 1860, he came to Boston to superintend the publication of one of his works, and remained there until his death, which took place June 21, 1866. He was an earnest and laborious student in his profession, in which he gained distinction as an instructor.

Miss Hosea, Isaac Brooks, Esq., and Mr. Eli Wilkins were among the early teachers in the schools of Amherst. Miss Hosea seems to have been inclined to take life easily. I have the authority of one of her pupils, who was afterwards for a long time one of "ye fathers of ye towne," for saying, that after she had heard her pupils through their lessons, she would request them to be good children while she took a nap; but while the teacher slept, the wide awake pupils, the father aforesaid included, employed themselves in chasing squirrels on the log fences, or stoning the red-headed woodpeckers, which then abounded on the chestnut stubs standing in the fields near by. A dark colored slate stone, standing near the south-west corner of the new cemetery, marks the resting-place of this pioneer teacher. On it we read the inscription,—"Miss Mercy Hosea, died August 3, 1838, aged 95."

Isaac Brooks, Esq., was born in Woburn, Mass., August 16,

1757. He had the reputation of being an excellent teacher, excelling particularly in penmanship, as an examination of the county records from 1805 to 1828 will show. He married Abigail Kendrick, a sister of the mother of Gen. Pierce, and died December 21, 1840.

Eli Wilkins, Esq., served on the board of selectmen eight years, commencing with 1781. He was an excellent penman. While teaching school he evidently did his best to keep out of harm's way himself, and guard against any unnecessary bloodshed among his pupils, one of whom (perhaps his testimony should be taken with some grains of allowance) used to say, that master Wilkins would, after putting on his coat and hat, open the door, and, having secured a way of escape for himself, dismiss his disciples with the injunction to let any killing that might be done be done accidentally. They were then left to "fight it out" at their leisure.

I think that few complaints were made of frequent changes in text-books used in the schools in those times. The Testament and Æsop's Fables, the last adorned with marvellous wood-cuts, furnished the older pupils with reading matter; Dilworth and Cocker furnished the arithmetics; while Perry's Spelling-book and the New England Primer, containing the shorter catechism and the lamentable account of "ye burning of Mr. John Rogers," delighted the hearts and eyes of the youngest of the flock.

Strange visitors sometimes put in an appearance at these old-fashioned temples of science. On one occasion a house adder, of fair proportions, was discovered on the plate of the old school-house, in the Campbell district, in close proximity to the teacher's head. A confusion of tongues ensued, and, after a vigorous application of clubs and the broomstick, the intruder was slain, to the great edification of the company.

Samuel Wilkins, son of the first minister, was one of the three deacons elected January 10, 1774. He served on the board of selectmen fifteen years, and was town-clerk ten years. He seems to have been a stout muscular man in his prime, abounding in life and good humor. Like his father he became very infirm in his old age, but was tenderly cared for by his sons Daniel and Thomas. In his youth he delighted in feats of strength and agility, and but few were found who could master him in wrestling. Many anecdotes are told of him, showing his wit and good humor. On one occasion a boy, belonging to a family whose reputation for veracity was not very good, appeared before him very much frightened, saying he had seen a bear in the woods near by. "What sort of a tail had he?" said the deacon. "A long bushy one," said the boy. "Is your name Pike?" quoth the deacon. "Yes." "Go right along, the bear won't hurt you."

When a little past middle life he had the misfortune to lose his wife, a most estimable woman, who left him with a large family of little ones. After a proper time had elapsed, he sought another partner, and, after making himself agreeable as possible to the chosen one, he one day asked if she thought of going to heaven. Somewhat surprised, she answered that she hoped to. So do I, said our deacon—what say you to making the rest of the journey with me? Not being denied, a very pleasant journey of some forty-four years' duration commenced shortly after.

John Hubbard Wilkins, youngest son of Dea. Wilkins, graduated at Harvard college, 1818, was for a long time a publisher and stationer in Boston, and at one time the "whig" candidate for mayor of that city. He was one of the first in this country to accept the views of Baron Swedenborg, and was for a long time an active member and supporter of the Church of the New Jerusalem, in Boston.

George Wilkins Kendall, a grandson of Dea. Wilkins, was born in the old north-west parish, now Mont Vernon. He spent a good portion of his boyhood at his grandfather's, and is remembered by those who attended school in the old "Taylor" district, at that time, as the wag of the school, abounding in sallies of wit and good-natured mischief. He was one of the originators, and for some time editor-in-chief of the New Orleans *Picayune*. He travelled in nearly every state of the Union, and was a member of the ill-starred Santa Fé expedition in 1841. After the close of the war with Mexico, he went to Texas, and engaged in sheep raising. He died there some years since.

Another of the deacons of happy memory, who would have delighted the heart of Parson Murray, was the second Dea. Seaton, a native of the town, born (so says the town book) April

8, 1756. His family was originally from Scotland. On the overthrow of the Stuarts, to whose fortunes the Seatons adhered, their estates were confiscated and the family dispersed. John and Andrew Seaton went to Tellahoage, Ireland. Some years after, John came to New England, and settled in Boxford, Mass., 1729. Andrew sailed for Boston ten years later, with his family, and lost his wife in the wreck of the ship. He reached Boxford in 1740. John, son of John, married Ismenia, daughter of Andrew, and settled in Amherst. He was elected deacon January 10, 1774, and held the office till he removed to Washington, N. H., 1787. He was a man of genuine worth—the father of Ann Seaton, who married Hon. John Duncan, of Antrim, and of Dea. John Seaton, the subject of our notice, who was endowed with the gift of song. His ear delighted in the sounds of the viol and harp, and in his youth he was chief among the dancers. In his mature life he was for a long time the leader among the singers in the sanctuary.

I remember him as an old man who generally came late to meeting, riding with his aged companion in an ancient chaise, which might have suggested the legend of "ye Deacon's one-horse shay" to Dr. Holmes. After securing his horse, he would make his way up the broad aisle to "ye deacon's seat," his progress being announced by a pair of desperately creaking boots. His nose, of imperial dimensions, which would have excited the admiration of the first Napoleon, and won for its owner the decoration of the grand legion of honor at sight, was the source of much amusement to him. Being seated at table one day, a stranger, who sat opposite him, suggested rather angrily that the application of a handkerchief to it would be a benefit. Ever ready to oblige, the deacon handed him the handkerchief, with the request that he would attend to it, as he was nearer the offending member than its owner. A good understanding between the parties was arrived at at once.

Meeting the mail carrier, Wheat, one day, who, for some reason, disliked him, the deacon seized Wheat's nose, which rivalled his own in size, with his left hand, turning it as far as he could from him, at the same time turning his head half round to the right, he said—"I think, brother Wheat, that we can pass one another." "With charity for all, bearing malice towards none," the good deacon passed through life, and "fell asleep" October 3, 1836.

Jonathan Hildreth, son of Jacob, born August 12, 1767, was for a long time a noted teacher of music in Amherst. For some years he was the chorister at the meeting-house. Being something of a mechanic, he constructed several bass viols, some of which were used to aid in the services of the choir. He died July 4, 1816. His cousin, Benjamin Kendrick, was afterwards leader of the choir, and was noted for his skill in music. He died December 15, 1853, aged 74.

In the army which took Quebec in 1759 was a youth of fifteen winters, named Henry Cod. After the close of the war he obtained some knowledge of medicine, and engaged in practice in Amherst. Adding another syllable to his name, he became Dr. Codman. He seems to have possessed naturally a good stock of common sense, and had some skill in his profession, but was rough and eccentric in his manner. Towards the close of his life he indulged far too frequently in the use of what the fathers called strong waters. Many anecdotes of a ludicrous character are related of him. On one occasion he was called to visit a young lady belonging to one of the first families, who had been severely wounded in the neck by being thrown from a carriage. She was well covered with blood when the healer entered the room, "well set up." "Well, Sal," quoth he, "you look like a great stuck pig" (the adjectives in the original omitted).

Speaking of the doctors in Amherst, he said there were quite too many. "There are but four," was the answer. "There are a thousand," said Esculapius. "How do you make that out?" "There's me, I am one; there's S., he's a cypher; there's C., another cypher; and N., another one; and one and three cyphers make a thousand, don't they?"

One time when the dysentery prevailed in town, the doctor was very successful in saving his patients. Other practitioners were not so fortunate, and lost nearly all. A good old lady, who was much among the sick, noticed that whenever he was called he left pills of an enormous size, giving directions that one, two, or three, or as many as the patient felt inclined to take, should be administered at a time—the more the better. After the sickly season was over, the good lady asked him what the pills were made of. "Rye meal," said the doctor, "the best thing in the world for the dysentery."

Having taken "a drop too much," before starting on a professional trip one day, his horse stumbled and speedily unloaded his master, with the attendant saddle-bags. The medicines contained in the saddle-bags were badly mixed. So, stirring them all together, he administered doses of the compound with great success, performing wonderful cures, to his great delight. Speaking of it to a friend, the friend suggested that he had better prepare another dose similar to the one he had just used up. "I would do it," said the doctor, "but I'll be hanged if I know the right proportions of the medicines."

Being summoned one day to visit an old lady in the northerly part of the town, he told some boys he met that he was going up to kill old Goody S. She was seventy-six years old, and had no business to live any longer. For his part, he did not mean to live so long as that; would kill himself first. As good as his word, he died March 14, 1812, aged sixty-eight years.

In the longevity of its inhabitants, I think Amherst compares favorably with other towns of equal size. I have in my possession a list of one hundred and forty-four persons who have here deceased since January 1, 1823. Of them, one hundred and five were between eighty and ninety years; thirty-six between ninety and one hundred years; and three over one hundred years of age.

The oldest person of whom I have any record, who has died in town, was Mrs. Hepsibah Hartshorn, daughter of Eben and Lydia Holt, from whom Holt's meadow derives its name. She was born June 13, 1747, and died January 11, 1851, at the age of one hundred and three years, six months, and twenty-eight days. She had been a cripple for many years, walking by the aid of a crutch; yet she milked her cow after she had passed her ninety-fifth year. For some years before her death her hearing was much impaired. She occupied a log house,—the last of its kind, I think, in town,—which was taken down after her death.

Mrs. Mary Barnard was born at Lancaster, Mass., March 29, 1722, and died here October 13, 1823. She was a daughter of Jeremiah Holman, and was married to Robert Barnard, of Bolton, Mass. One of her sons was Rev. Jeremiah Barnard, the second minister of Amherst. Her daughter, Miss Lydia Barnard, born at Bolton, Mass., October 6, 1757, died in Amherst, September 17, 1859, lacking but a few days of one hundred and two years. A granddaughter, Mrs. Betsy King, daughter of Rev. Jeremiah Barnard, died at Rockdale, Iowa, January 14, 1872, aged ninety-six years, six months, and eleven days.

Daniel Campbell, Esq., the oldest man who has ever deceased in Amherst, was born in Londonderry, now Windham, N. H., June 27, 1739; settled in Amherst in 1760, where he resided until his death, which took place October 7, 1838. In his active life he was one of the leading citizens of the town, serving as moderator at the annual town-meeting, selectman for many years, and representative. Possessed of a strong will, an iron constitution, and energy enough for a dozen men, his strength and faculties held out remarkably to the last. In his old age he was quite a politician. He attended and voted at the town-meeting the spring before his death.

Jenny Hylands, to whom he was married, June 25, 1760, was a few months older than her husband, and a native of Londonderry. She was a woman of rare energy and excellence; one in whom "the heart of her husband did safely trust." She literally "made linen, and sold it. She looked well to the ways of her household, and ate not the bread of idleness. Her husband praised her. Her children also arise up and call her blessed." She died November 25, 1815, aged seventy-seven.

This family, consisting of five members, is remarkable for longevity,—the father dying at the age of ninety-nine, the mother at seventy-seven, their son at seventy-five, their eldest daughter at eighty-two, and their youngest daughter at ninety-two; an average of eighty-five years.

The oldest person who ever lived in town is Mrs. Anah Goss, who will complete her one hundred and fourth year on the 1st day of February, 1874.

According to the census of 1870, there were eighty-two persons in town over seventy years of age. Of these, fifty-nine were between seventy and eighty; twenty-two between eighty and ninety; and one over one hundred years.

The eldest male native of Amherst, now living, is probably

Mr. Uriah Wilkins,* son of Aaron and Lydia Smith Wilkins, who completed his eighty-fifth year, November 4, 1873. Two of his brothers have deceased,—one aged eighty-four years and four months, the other aged seventy years and one month; one is still living, aged eighty-three years and three months. Two sisters have deceased,—one at the age of eighty-six years and two months, the other aged seventy-five years and four months; one is now living, aged seventy-nine years and seven months. Average age of the members of the family at the present time, eighty and four sevenths years.

But I trespass too long upon your patience. Our town and its people have a history of which no one need be ashamed. Generations of patriotic, noble-hearted men, and chaste, loving women, have here lived and passed away. Their memories are blessed. Let it be our endeavor so to live, that the record of the sons and daughters of old Amherst, handed down to us, shall be transmitted without spot or blemish to our successors.

To the foregoing description of former citizens, by Mr. Secomb, I append a list of the officers of the church, with such facts relating to their lives and characters as I have been able to gather since the discourse was written; also, a list of all the graduates at colleges from Amherst, so far as I have been able to ascertain the names.

J. G. DAVIS.

DEACONS OF THE FIRST CONGREGATIONAL CHURCH IN AMHERST.

Humphrey Hobbs, the first in this office, was elected January 6, 1743. He was a man of great personal courage, having the true instincts of a soldier. His success in the conflict with the Indians in Amherst seems to have led him to enter the volunteer service in defence of the province. He was captain of a

---

* Mr. Wilkins died early in April, 1874.

company, stationed at Charlestown, No. 4, and in that capacity exhibited superior qualities in skirmishes with the Indians.

Joseph Boutell, the second deacon, was elected June 3, 1743. From an obituary notice, published in the first volume of the *Amherst Journal*, I learn that "he served in this office fifty-two years, during which his exemplary behaviour rendered him an honor and an ornament to the holy profession he had made and the office he sustained, and secured for him the respect and esteem of all who knew him." He died May 19, 1795, in his eighty-ninth year.

Third—James Cochran was elected deacon in 1744, to fill the vacancy made by the resignation of Dea. Hobbs. I have not been able to learn his origin. He held the office, enjoying the confidence of his brethren, till his death, January 5, 1774.

On the 10th January, 1774, a meeting of the church, "duly notified," was held for "the purpose of choosing several brethren into the sacred office of deacon," when, by a major part of the votes taken, Mr. Samuel Wilkins, Mr. John Seaton, and Mr. Nahum Baldwin were chosen into said office. This election was consequent on the death of Dea. Cochran, and the fresh interest awakened by the completion of the new meeting-house. All these persons are mentioned elsewhere, and in connections that prove that they were men of vigorous sense and practical talents, asserting a decided influence among their townsmen in the agitation and debates of that stirring period. Dea. Wilkins resigned his office in 1816.

On the 18th of June, 1788, Dea. Baldwin, having died in May, and Dea. Seaton having removed from town the preceding year, Mr. Ephraim Barker and Mr. Joshua Lovejoy "were chosen into the office" of deacons.

Dea. Barker was widely known as a man of business, and a superior mechanic. He was twice married,—had a large and interesting family, and was highly respected by the community. He was distinct and tenacious in the expression of his theological opinions. Being an excellent singer, he acted as chorister in the church for many years. He was a native of Rockingham county; born in or near Exeter, 1732, and died September 29, 1800.

Joshua Lovejoy and his wife brought letters from the Second

church in Andover, Mass., on which they were admitted to this church April 22, 1781. He was a man of fair talents, without much education. Served as selectman and town clerk in the years 1790–1794. He removed from town soon after, and died at Sanbornton, January 28, 1832, at the age of eighty-eight.

"On the 3d September, 1795, Dea. Boutell having deceased, and Dea. Lovejoy having left town," Mr. Amos Elliott, born June 17, 1755, son of Francis, and John Seaton, son of John, born April 8, 1756, were chosen deacons. Dea. Seaton is described on page 68, and, notwithstanding his peculiarities, was a valuable citizen. Dea. Elliott was a farmer, of retiring manners, but highly esteemed as a consistent Christian. After his death, April 7, 1807, John Hartshorn, born June 21, 1759, second son of James, who came to Amherst late in the autumn of 1764, from Reading, Mass., was elected deacon September 1, 1808. Like Dea. Elliott, whom he succeeded, he was by occupation a farmer, and a man of few words. In personal appearance he was a man of dignity, as became the office, in which he purchased a good degree, being a man of sound judgment and real Christian worth. He continued in office till his death, November 28, 1842.

In the spring of 1816, Richard Boylston, David Holmes, Edmund Parker, with their wives, united with the church, and several ineffectual efforts were made to persuade these gentlemen and others to accept the office of deacon. In one case, if not more, the candidate was elected in anticipation of his becoming a member of the church. After the installation of Dr. Lord as pastor, the objections previously entertained were removed, and Matthias Spalding and David Holmes consented to serve.

Dr. Spalding, born at Chelmsford, Mass., June 25, 1769, graduated at Harvard college, 1798, commenced practice in Amherst, 1806, where he gained a wide reputation as a skilful physician and surgeon; was elected deacon May 29, 1817, and continued in office till his death, May 22, 1865. Through life he was distinguished for his fine social qualities, gentlemanly deportment, and steadfast support of religious institutions. In times of difficulty he was a good counsellor, and by his considerate management was often of great service to the church in maintaining discipline. For a more complete statement of his character, as a citizen, an esteemed and honored member of the medical profession, and other particulars of his long and useful life, see Spalding Memorial, pp. 79–83.

David Holmes, who was elected deacon at the same time, after a few years, in 1823, resigned his office, as his views of religious doctrine were not in harmony with the prevailing sentiment in the church. He became an active member of the Christian society, and, on his removal from town, settled at Lowell, Mass.

Amos Elliott, son of Amos, and the second deacon of that name, was elected November 1, 1823. He is represented as a man of slight figure, a skilful musician, fond of books, and often employed in teaching school. He held the office three years, dying in 1826, at the age of fifty-two. The name and services of the Elliotts, father and son, are pleasantly associated with those of Dea. Hartshorn, in the cherished remembrances of the neighborhood in which they lived, generally designated as "Christian Hill."

Edmund Parker was born at Jaffrey, February 7, 1783; graduated at Dartmouth college, 1803. Came to Amherst, where he studied law. Opened a law office in 1807, and soon gained distinction in his profession. He was a thorough student of the Scriptures, and his life was penetrated and directed by its precepts. Elected deacon May 15, 1832. He retained the office until his removal to Nashua in 1836. He is described by Dr. Edward Spalding "as a representative man, to whose wisdom and prudence others willingly deferred. In social and public meetings he was conspicuously active and influential,—especially in seasons of unusual religious interest, when his sound judgment and devout piety made him a true colleague to his pastor, and a paternal helper to those seeking the way of life. Under a natural sedateness and gravity of manner, which to a stranger indicated something of sternness, there glowed a warm and generous heart, full of kindly impulses, and ever ready for some good word or work. He loved the society of the young, and in his advanced years retained the playfulness of a boy. Few men take as much pains as he did to encourage and lend a helping hand to those beginning the struggle of life. Take him for all in all, he filled with rare completeness the measure of a Christian gentleman's life." He was a trustee of Dartmouth college from 1828 to 1856. On his removal to Nashua he was chosen deacon in the Olive Street church, and continued in office till the time of his death, which occurred at Claremont, while on a visit to his daughter, Mrs. Prentiss, September 8, 1856.

Abel Downe, born November 2, 1788. Came to Amherst from Fitchburg, Mass., about the year 1832. Chosen deacon January 21, 1836, and continued in office till his death, September 28, 1840. He is described as a man of quiet manners and genial spirit, a trustworthy citizen and devoted Christian. He was much esteemed by all who knew him.

David Fisk, 3d, born at Merrimack, September 12, 1792, was elected deacon Nov. 18, 1836. A man of commanding presence, vigorous mind, and decided opinions. He was prompt and true in meeting the calls of duty. He was firm in the expression of his religious sentiments, but, practically, benevolent and kind. Having served in this office with an upright and zealous Christian character for twenty-three years, he removed to Nashua in 1860, where he died, after an honored old age, June 22, 1873. For details of his life, see history of the Fiske family, p. 156.

Cyrus Eastman, born May 7, 1787, at Concord, of a race distinguished for the substantial qualities of energy, prudence, and piety, was chosen deacon December 30, 1836. Naturally impulsive, and almost indifferent to his own pecuniary advantage, he was humble and hearty in his devotion to the welfare of the church. Averse to strife, he shared his full proportion of all the burdens of society, fulfilling the duties of his office with reverence and fidelity until the end of his life, December 17, 1862. See *Farmer's Cabinet*, December 25, 1862.

Aaron Lawrence, born in Hollis, December 3, 1803, was trained in a store for mercantile pursuits. Tall, but slight in figure, he was never robust in health. Naturally timid and distrustful, he persisted, in obedience to the calls of duty, till he acquired character and influence. He united with the church early in life, and for many years was the only young man in it. He was a cordial supporter of the ministry, thoughtful and friendly to the young and the homeless, generous to the needy, and a liberal patron of all Christian enterprises. Elected deacon

November 2, 1860. He held the office till his death, September 1, 1867, when a sermon was preached delineating his character. His attachment to the church and the town was manifested by valuable legacies.

In reviewing the names of these officers, it is manifest that this church has been highly favored in the consistent and trustworthy character of its deacons. The larger portion of this number were men of intelligence and superior understanding,—illustrating in their lives the principles of the New Testament. Three fourths of the catalogue attained to an unusual age, confirming the declaration of the Psalmist,—"Those that be planted in the house of the Lord shall flourish in the courts of our God. They shall bring forth fruit in old age. They shall be fat and flourishing, to show that the Lord is upright."

The present officers of the church are,—Barnabas B. David, elected January 2, 1845; Edward D. Boylston, elected April 12, 1860; Charles H. David, elected November 2, 1871.

GRADUATES AT COLLEGE FROM AMHERST.

AT HARVARD COLLEGE.

NAME.	DATE.	PROFESSION.
*John Wilkins,	1774,	Instructor.
*Jacob Kimball,	1788,	Farmer.
*Charles H. Atherton,	1794,	Lawyer.
*Daniel Weston,	1795,	Clergyman.
*William Gordon,	1806,	Lawyer.
*James F. Dana,	1813,	Physician.
*Samuel L. Dana,	1813,	Physician.
*John H. Wilkins,	1818,	Bookseller.
*Charles G. Atherton,	1822,	Lawyer.
*Stephen R. Holmes,	1822,	Instructor.

* Deceased.

AT DARTMOUTH COLLEGE.

NAME.	DATE.	PROFESSION.
*Reuben D. Mussey,	1803,	Physician.
*Benjamin F. French,	1812,	Lawyer.
*James McK. Wilkins,	1812,	Lawyer.
*Levi Hartshorn,	1813,	Clergyman.
Allen Fisk,	1814,	Instructor.
*Samuel Whiting,	1818,	Lawyer.
Charles F. Elliott,	1829,	Physician.
Edward Spalding,	1833,	Physician.
Charles E. Parker,	1834,	Physician.
William Read,	1839,	Physician.
*Edward H. Pratt,	1841,	Physician.
Alfred Spalding,	1843,	Physician.
Edward Aiken,	1851,	Physician.
John H. Clark,	1857,	Physician.
*Charles H. Wallace,	1857,	Studied Law.
Vaola J. Hartshorn,	1860,	Clergyman.
Warren Upham,	1871,	Civil Engineer.

AT BOWDOIN COLLEGE.

NAME.	DATE.	PROFESSION.
*Robert Means,	1807,	Lawyer.
*William Appleton,		Lawyer.
*James Means,	1833,	Clergyman.

AT AMHERST COLLEGE.

NAME.	DATE.	PROFESSION.
William O. Baldwin,	1851,	Clergyman.
John E. Wheeler,	1857,	Clergyman.
Wm. B. Clark,	1865,	Banker.

AT WILLIAMS COLLEGE.

NAME.	DATE.	PROFESSION.
Edward C. David,	1850,	Lawyer.
William G. David,	1852,	Physician.

* Deceased.

The following documents, from authentic sources, may possess some interest to those who are curious in such matters.

S.

On the 16th of March, 1621, the inhabitants of Plymouth, Mass., were alarmed at seeing a sturdy Indian walk into their settlement, and, passing by the houses, go directly where the people were collected. He saluted them in broken English, and bade them welcome. He was affable; told them his dwelling was five days' travel from thence, and that he was a sagamore or prince. He understood the geography of the country; gave an account of the different tribes, their sagamores, and number of men. They kindly entertained him, and gave him a horseman's coat. He tarried all night, and received, on going away, a knife, a bracelet, and a ring, and promised in a few days to return again. He returned, according to promise, and brought five others with him. They sung and danced, and were very friendly and familiar.

The 22d of March *Samoset* came again, and brought *Squande* with him, who had been carried to Spain and sold there; but, escaping, had made his way to London, and from thence to America. Three others accompanied them, and gave information that Massasoit,—one of the most powerful sagamores of the neighboring Indians,—was near. He soon appeared on the top of a hill near by, accompanied by sixty men. Edward Winslow was sent to treat with him, carrying presents of jewelry, food, and strong water. After receiving the presents, they were desired to visit the governor, who received them with drum and trumpet sounding, and other military parade. A green rug and three or four cushions were spread for the company. The governor kissed the king's hand, and the king his, and both sat down. "Strong water" was then given the king, who drank a great draught that made him sweat all the while after. Victuals were then set before them. Massasoit at this meeting entered into a formal and very friendly treaty with the English, wherein they agreed to avoid injuries on both sides, to punish offenders, to restore stolen goods, to assist each other in all justifiable wars, to promote peace among their neighbors, &c.

Massasoit and his successors, for forty years, inviolably observed this treaty, and the English were much indebted to him for his friendship.

In 1662, Alexander, the son and successor of Massasoit, jealous of the growing power of the English, invited the Narragansetts,—a powerful tribe,—to join with him in revolting from the English. Learning this, Gen. Winslow went with ten men and brought him to Plymouth, where, though he was treated very civilly, his vexation and madness threw him into a fever, of which he died. His brother Philip succeeded him, and renewed the covenant with the English; yet, in 1671, he commenced hostilities against them, but was soon subdued, and promised never to begin war again before he had made complaint himself to Plymouth colony.

In 1674 one John Sassamon, an Indian whom the settlers employed as a missionary to instruct his brethren, informed the governor that Philip and several other sachems were plotting the destruction of the English. Soon after this Sassamon was found murdered. Three Indians were arrested, tried, convicted, and hung for the murder. Philip, much offended at this, sent away his women, armed his men, and robbed several houses of the settlers in the vicinity of his own dwelling.

June 24, 1675, the colony observed as a day of humiliation and prayer. As the people of Swanzey were returning from public worship, the Indians, lying in ambush, fired a volley, killing one man and wounding another. Two persons who went for a surgeon were shot, and in another part of the town six persons more were killed.

The war thus commenced raged fiercely through the summer and autumn of that year. Finally the Indians were defeated in a fight at Hatfield, and sought shelter on a small piece of dry land, surrounded by a great swamp. There they fortified themselves as well as they were able, and awaited the onset of the English, which was made December 19, 1675, and resulted in the total defeat and overthrow of the Indians,—probably 1,000 of their number being slain, or dying of wounds received in the battle. The victory was, however, dearly bought by the conquerors, a large number of whom were slain. Philip escaped, and with his remaining warriors did much mischief. Finally, being closely pursued by the English, he took refuge in a swamp, where he was shot through the heart by an Indian, August 12, 1676. His head was sent to Plymouth, where it was received on the day they had devoted to solemn thanksgiving.

Never, says the historian, has New England seen so dismal a period as the war with Philip. About 600 men,—the flower of her strength,—had fallen in battle. There were few families who had not lost some near relation. Twelve or thirteen towns had been utterly destroyed, and others greatly damaged. About 600 buildings, chiefly dwelling-houses, had been burned, and a large debt contracted. About every eleventh family had been burned out, and an eleventh part of the militia slain. So costly is the inheritance we have received from our fathers.

With the avowed intention of rewarding the soldiers who served in this war, coupled probably with the desire to strengthen their claim to the government and soil of New Hampshire, the general court of Massachusetts, at its session in June, 1728, made the following grant:

At a Great and General Court or Assembly for His Majesty's Province of the Massachusetts Bay, in New England, Begun and holden at Boston, the 29th day of May, 1728.

June 15, 1728, In the House of Representatives.

In answer to the Petition of the Soldiers that served in the Narraganset War. Resolved, That Major Chandler, Mr. Edward Shove, Major Tilestone, and Mr. John Hobson (or any three of them) be a Committee, fully authorized and empowered to survey and lay out two tracts of land for townships, of the contents of six miles square each, in some of the unappropriated Land of this Province; and that the said lands be granted and disposed of to the persons, whether Officers or Soldiers, belonging to this Province, who were in the service of their country in the said Narraganset War, or to their lawful Representatives, as a reward for their public services; and is in full satisfaction of the Grant formerly made them by the Great and General Court. And forasmuch as it is the full Intent and Purpose of this Court, that every Officer and Soldier should have a compensation made him over and above what wages and gratuities any of them have already received.

That Public Notice be given in the News Letters, and advertisements be posted up in every Town in the Province, notifying all Persons that now survive and that were in that fight, and the legal Representatives of those deceased, that they give or send a list of their names and descents to this Court at their next fall session; and when such list is completed, by a Committee then to be appointed by this Court, the Grantees shall be obliged to assemble in as short a time as they can conveniently, not exceeding six months, and proceed to the choice of a Committee to regulate each Propriety, who shall pass such orders and rules as will oblige them effectually to settle sixty families at least in each Township, with a learned Orthodox minister, within the space of seven years from the date of the Grant. PROVIDED, nevertheless, That if said Grantees shall not effectually settle the said number of families in each Township, and also lay out a lot of land for the first settled minister,—One for the Ministry, and one for the school in each of said Townships,—they shall have no advantage, but forfeit their said Grants, any thing to the contrary herein contained notwithstanding.

Exd. pr. Thads. Mason, Dep. Sec'y.

In Council read and concurred. Consented to.

William Dummer.

A true copy. Attest: Samuel Kneeland, Clerk.

June 8, 1732.

In the House of Representatives, Voted: to allow a further grant of land to the Officers and Soldiers who were in the Narraganset fight, so that every 120 persons whose claims had been or should be allowed within four months from that date, should have a Township of the contents of six miles square; and that the same Committee, who laid out the two first Townships, should lay out the remainder at the expense of the Province.

Concurred in by the Council, June 9, 1732.

J. Willard, Secy.

Apr. 20, 1733. Approved, J. BELCHER, Gov.

The whole number of persons whose claims were allowed, being eight hundred and forty, an act was passed June 30, 1732, granting them 5 additional townships. This act was concurred in by the Council, July 4, 1732, and approved by Gov. Belcher, April 26, 1733.

All the grantees, or their representatives, assembled on Boston Common, June 6, 1733, at which time they divided themselves into seven distinct societies, of 120 persons, each society being entitled to one township. Three persons were chosen from each society, who, on the 17th of October, 1733, assigned the several townships among their respective societies. No. 3, afterwards called Souhegan West No. 3, was assigned to the Salem Society, which consisted of the following persons:

SALEM.

John Harradway's heirs,	Thomas Bell,
John Elwell,	Jonathan Lambert,
John Rabson,	William Osburn,
Thomas Putnam,	John Bullock,
Nathaniel Soams,	Jeremiah Neal,
Robert Hutchinson,	John Gloyd,
Ezekiel Marsh,	Habbakuk Gardner,
William Fuller,	John Abbott,
Jonathan Marsh,	Thomas Keney's heirs,
Jonathan Verry,	Edward Hollis' heirs,
Joseph Holton,	Joseph Prince,
John Flynt,	John Tarbell's heirs,
Samuel Pickworth's heirs,	Thomas Larkin,
William Curtis,	Samuel Manning's heirs.
John Trask,	

MARBLEHEAD.

William Hind,	Thomas Martin,
Richard Shapley,	Joseph Sweat,
Jonathan Wolcott,	Jeremiah Getchel.
Joseph Majory,	

LYNN.

Henry Collins,	Samuel Greaves,
John Newhall,	Samuel Edmonds,
Thomas Baker,	John Farrington,
William Bassett,	Michael Bowden,

Richard Johnson,
William Collins,
Ebenezer Burrill,
Benjamin Potter,
Joseph Farr,
Benjamin Ramsdell,
Ruth Driver,
Samuel Newhall,
John Ballard,
Richard Moor,
Joseph Farr,
Robert Rand,
Edmond Lewis,
Samuel Tarbox's heirs,
Jonathan Johnson,
Ebenezer Burrill,
Timothy Breed,
Andrew Townsend's heirs,
Joseph Haven.

GLOUCESTER.

Jacob Row,
Samuel Ingersoll,
Edw. Harrington,
John Day,
Samuel Stevens.

ANDOVER.

Ebenezer Tyler,
James Fry,
William Ballard,
John Presson,
John Ballard,
Ebenezer Barker,
Andrew Peters,
John Parker.

TOPSFIELD.

Zaccheus Perkins,
Nathaniel Wood,
Moses Pingreese,
Abraham Fitts' heirs,
Thomas Davis' heirs,
Elihu Wardwell's heirs,
John Hutchins' heirs,
Josiah Clark's heirs,
James Ford's heirs,
Samuel Perkins' heirs,
Joseph Herrick,
Jonathan Wilds' heirs,
Samuel Kneeland,
Samuel Kneeland.

BEVERLY.

Thomas Rayment,
Ralph Elinwood,
Henry Bayley,
Christopher Reed,
Lot Conant,
Thomas Blackfield,
Andrew Dodge,
Joseph Morgan,
William Dodge's heirs,
John Dodge's heirs,
Jonathan Byells,
William Rayment's heirs,
Joseph Pickett,
Samuel Harris' heirs.

WENHAM.

Thomas Abbott,
Elizabeth Fowler,
John Batchelder,
William Rogers,
Thomas Perkins.

BOXFORD.

Stephen Peabody,
James Curtis,
John Andrews,
John Bixbe.

BRADFORD.

Ichabod Boynton.

SCARBOROUGH.

John Harmon.

READING.

John Bowtell,
Thomas Bancroft.

YORK.

Denison Sargent.

FALMOUTH.

Joseph Hatch,
Philip Dexter.

CHATHAM.

Robert Nicholson.

The first meeting of the grantees of Narraganset No. 3, or Souhegan West, was held at Salem village, now Danvers, July 17, 1734; and their first meeting within the limits of the township was held at the meeting-house, January 30, 1745.

The first settlement of the town was probably made in the spring of 1735, by Samuel Walton and Samuel Lampson, on the place now occupied by Mr. Bryant Melendy. Walton died in Amherst. None of his descendants remain here. Lampson died in Billerica, but his children remained in Amherst, where some of their descendants still reside.

CHARTER OF AMHERST—1760.

PROVINCE OF NEW HAMPSHIRE.

George the Second, by the Grace of God, of Great Britain, France, and Ireland, King, Defender of Faith:

To all to whom these Presents shall come. Greeting.

Whereas our Loyal subjects, Inhabitants of a Tract of Land within our Province of New Hampshire, known by the name of Souhegan West, on the western side of Merrimac, have humbly petitioned and requested us that they may be erected and Incorporated into a Township, and Infranchised with the same powers and priveleges which other Towns within our said Province by law have and enjoy. And it appearing to us to be conducive to the general good of our said Province, as well as of the said Inhabitants in particular, by maintaining good order and encouraging the culture of the land, that the same should be done. Know Ye, therefore, that We, of our special Grace, certain knowledge, and for the encouragement and promoting of the good ends aforesaid, By and with the advice of our trusty and well beloved Benning Wentworth, Esq., our Governor and Commander-in-chief, and of our Council for said province of New Hampshire, Have erected and ordained, and by these Presents for us, our heirs and successors, Do Will and ordain that the Inhabitants of the Tract of land aforesaid, and who shall inhabit and improve thereon hereafter, the same being Butted and Bounded as follows: Viz., Beginning at Souhegan River; thence running North, 1 degree West, on the townships of Merrimac and Bedford, six miles; thence running west on Bedford and a tract of land called New Boston, six miles; thence South about five miles and a half to Souhegan River aforesaid; thence by said River to the place where it began; Be, and hereby are, declared and ordained to be a Town Corporate, and are hereby erected and Incorporated into a body Politic and Corporate, to to have continuance until the first of January, 1762, by the name of Amherst, with all the Powers and Authorities, Privileges, Immunities, and Franchises which any other Towns in said Province, by Law, hold and enjoy to the said inhabitants, or who shall hereafter inhabit there, and their successors, for said term, always reserving to us, our Heirs and Successors, all White Pine trees that are, or shall be found growing, and being on said tract of land fit for the use of our Royal Navy; Reserving also to us, our Heirs and successors, the power and the right of dividing said town, when it shall appear necessary and convenient to the Inhabitants thereof. Provided, nevertheless, and it is hereby declared, that this Charter and Grant is not intended, and shall not in any manner be construed to extend to, or affect the Private Property of the soil within the limits aforesaid. And as the several towns within our said Province aforesaid are by the laws thereof enabled and authorized to assemble, and by the majority of voters present to choose all such officers, and transact such affairs as in the said laws are declared. We do, by these presents, nominate and appoint Lieut. Col. John Goffe to call the first meeting of said Inhabitants, to be held within said town, at any time within forty days from the date hereof, giving legal notice of the Time and design of holding such meeting. After which the annual meeting in said Town shall be held, for the choice of Officers and the purposes aforesaid, on the second Monday in March annually.

In testimony whereof we have caused the Seal of our Province to be hereunto affixed.

Witness—Benning Wentworth, Esquire, our Governor and Commander-in-Chief of our said Province, the eighteenth day of January, in the Thirty-Third year of our Reign, and in the Year of our Lord Christ, One thousand and seven hundred and sixty.

BENNING WENTWORTH.

By his Excellency's command, with advice of Council.

Theodore Atkinson, Secy.

Province of New Hampshire,

Recorded in the Book of Charters, page 212 and 213, this 19th day of January, 1760. pr.

THEODORE ATKINSON, Secy.

WARRANT FOR THE FIRST TOWN-MEETING.

FROM THE TOWN RECORDS.

Province of New Hampshire, January 21, 1760.

Notice is hereby given to all Persons Inhabiting that tract of Land formerly known by the name of Souhegan West, or Narraganset No. 3, that Whereas it has pleased his Excellency Gov. Wentworth, with the advice of the Council of this Province, to Incorporate the tract of land with the Inhabitants into a Township by the name of Amherst, and as it has pleased the said Governor and Council to nominate and appoint me, the subscriber, to call the first meeting for the choice of Town Officers.

These are, therefore, to Warn all the freeholders and other Inhabitants of said tract of Land now in the Town of Amherst, that they meet at the Meeting House in said town upon Wednesday, the Twentieth day of February next, at ten of the clock in the forenoon: To first, hear the Charter read; second, To choose all Town Officers for the Year ensuing, and till the second Tuesday of March in the Year 1761, as other Towns within this Province do.

Given under my hand this day and year above written.

JOHN GOFFE.

RECORD OF THE FIRST TOWN-MEETING.

Province of New Hampshire, February the 20th, 1760.

By virtue of a Charter, Granted by the Governor and Council of said Province, incorporating the tract of land, with the inhabitants of it, formerly known by the name of Souhegan West, into a town by the name of Amherst, and appointing Lieut. Col. John Goffe to call the first meeting for the choosing Town Officers for the ensuing year, by virtue of said charter I have called a meeting this twentieth day of February, 1760.

Upon said day the Inhabitants universally met, then without one contrary vote made choice of Solomon Hutchinson for Town Clerk, who was immediately sworn to the faithful execution of that office.

Voted, Col. John Goffe Moderator for said Meeting.

Voted, that the Charter is accepted.

Voted, that there shall be five Selectmen for the present year.

Voted, that these shall be Selectmen: Solomon Hutchinson, William Bradford, Reuben Mussey, Reuben Gould, Thomas Clark.

Voted, a Committee to examine the towns accounts: William Lancy, Benjamin Taylor, Thomas Wakefield.

Tythingmen, David Hartshorn, Nathan Kendall.

Voted, that the Selectmen be fence-viewers.

Clerk of the market, Thomas Wakefield.

Deer keepers, Joseph Steel, Joseph Prince, Will Lancy.

Field drivers, Nathan Fuller, Ebenezer Weston, Jr., James Seetown, James Rollins.

Constables, Ebenezer Weston, Joshua Abbott.

Surveyors of Highways, James Seetown, Ephraim Abbott, Samuel Stewart, Andrew Bradford, Will Lancy.

Voted, that the Selectmen shall be overseers of the poor for the present year.

Voted, Surveyor of lumber John Shepard, Jr.

These officers were sworn on said day to their several offices by John Goffe, Esq.

ASSOCIATION TEST OF 1776.

Copied from the original in the office of the Secretary of State, Concord, N. H.

TO THE SELECTMEN OF AMHERST.

In Committee of Safety, April 12, 1776.

In order to carry the underwritten Resolves of the Hon'ble Continental Congress into execution. You are requested to desire all males above Twenty One years of age (Lunaticks, Idiots, and Negroes excepted) to sign the declaration on this paper: and when so done, to make return hereof, together with the name or names of all who shall refuse to sign the same, to the General Assembly or Committee of Safety of this Colony.

M. WEARE, Chairman.

In Congress, March 14, 1776.

Resolved, that it be recommended to the several assemblies, Conventions, and Councils, or Committees of Safety of the United Colonies, immediately to cause all persons to be disarmed within their Respective Colonies, who are notoriously disaffected to the cause of America, or who have not associated, and refuse to associate, to defend by arms, the United Colonies against the hostile attempts of the British fleets and armies.

Extract from the minutes.

CHARLES THOMPSON, Secretary.

In consequence of the above resolution of the Hon. Continental Congress, and to show our determination in joining our American brethren in defending the Lives, Liberties, Properties of the Inhabitants of the United Colonies:—

We, the Subscribers, do hereby engage and promise, that we will, to the utmost of our power, at the risque of our Lives and Fortunes, with arms, oppose the Hostile proceedings of the British Fleets and Armies, against the United American Colonies.

Nahum Baldwin,	Henry Codman,	Henry Kimball,
Moses Nichols,	Peter Robinson,	William Low,
William Bradford,	Jona. Smith,	Samuel Stanley,
Josiah Crosby,	John Burns,	Jona. Grimes,
Peter Woodbury,	Stephen Washer,	Amos Flint,
Thomas Burns,	Samuel Harris,	William Read,
Robert Means,	David Hildreth,	Joseph Steel,
Nathan Jones,	Ephraim Barker,	William Odell,
Joseph Boutel,	Robert Reade,	Nathan Fuller,
Timothy Smith,	Samuel Hall,	John Dunklee,
Thomas Carell,	Archelaus Towne,	Amos Green,
Ephraim Hildreth,	Darius Abbott,	James Hartshorn,
Nathan Kendal,	Joseph Gould,	John Washer,
Benjamin Day,	Jona. Sawyer,	David Green,
Reuben Boutel,	Samson Crosby,	Phineas Upham,
Ebenezer Kea,	Nathl. Barrett, [Jr.,	John Shepard, Jun.,
Kendal Boutwel,	Nathan Hutchinson,	Simpson Steward,
Oliver Carlton,	John Grines,	Samuel Sterns?
Hezekiah Lovejoy,	Israel Towne, Jun.,	Dimond Mussey,
Enos Bradford,	William Taylor,	Moses Barron,

Thomas Towne,
Daniel Stephens,
James Seeton,
Benjamin Hopkins,
Jacob Curtice,
Jacob Curtice, Jr.,
Jonathan Taylor,
Josiah Dodge,
William Codman,
Silas Cummings,
Thomas McAlester,
Joseph Steel Jun.,
Timothy Nichols,
Benj. Hopkins, Jr.
Eben'r Hopkins,
John Burns,
Benj. Hartshorn,
John Seaton,
Willm. Wilkins,
Francis Lovejoy,
John Cochran,
James Gillmore,
Josiah Sawyer, Jr.,
Jona. Twiss,
Richard Hughes,
John Hartshorn,
Nathan Jones, Jun.,
Amos Flint, Jun.,
Saml. Stratton,
Nathan Hutchinson,
John Averill,
William Lamson,
John Cole,
Isaac Weston,
Nathan Cole,
Thomas Towne,
Joshua Wright,
Joshua Wilkins,
Thomas Clarke,

Jona. Lund,
Isaac Wright,
Benj. Kendrick,
Josiah Kidder,
William Peacock,
Joseph Pierce,
David Duncklee,
John Kendall, Jun.,
Isaac How,
Jacob Blodgett,
Adam Patterson,
Josiah Sawyer,
George Burns,
John Burns, Jun.,
Joseph Rollings,
Isaac Holt,
Joseph Cogin,
John Roby,
John Twiss,
James McKean,
Thos. Wakefield, Jr.,
Ebenr. Holt, Jun.,
Jona. Lamson,
Ephraim Abbot,
Moses Kimball,
Samuel Taylor,
Allen Goodridge,
Thos. Averill, Jun.,
Francis Elliott,
Elisha Felton,
Richard Ward,
Nathl. Haseltine,
Stephen Farnum,
William Wallace,
Peter C. Parker,
Andrew Bradford,
Stephen Burnham,
Abner Hutchinson,
David Truel ?

Benj. Merrill,
Jonathan Lyon,
William Hogg,
John Mitchell,
John Lovejoy,
Jacob Lovejoy,
Jacob Hildreth,
Samuel Henry,
John Patterson,
Joseph Prince, Junr.,
William Fisk, Jr.,
William Fisk,
Barthl. Dodge,
William Small,
Joseph Small,
William Small, Jun.,
Eben Hutchinson,
John Harwood,
John Tuck,
Willm. Peabody, Jr.,
Jona. Wilkins, Jun.,
John Seccombe,
Jacob Standly,
Willm. Peabody,
Joseph Boutwel,
Reuben Holt,
Michael Keef,
Joseph Prince,
Abijah Wilkins,
Thomas Weston,
Jacob Smith,
Ezekiel Upton,
Nathan Cleaves,
Joel Howe,
Stephen Peabody,
Willm. Odell, Jun.,
Ebenr. Temple,
Ephraim French,
Benjamin Dodge,

Lemuel Winchester, Israel Towne, James Gage,
Daniel Smith, John Bradford, Willm. Mellendy, Jr.,
Isaac Smith, Joseph Dunkley, Ebenr. Weston,
Nathan Flint, Ebenr. Averill, Richard Gould,
John Damon, Elisha Hutchinson, Saml. Blasdell,
James Woodbury, Joseph Farnum, Solomon Kittredge,
Benj. Temple, Amos Stickney, Timothy Hill,
Joseph Langdell, Joseph Wallace, John Wilkins.

To the Hon'ble The Committee of Safety, For the State of New Hampshire, or the General Assembly thereof:

Pursuant to the Request on this paper, from the Committee of Safety to us directed, we have invited those Persons therein named to sign the Declaration on this paper, and all that have seen it have signed it except Joshua Atherton, Esq., Mr. Daniel Campbell, Mr. Samuel Dodge, and Col. John Shepard.

THOMAS WAKEFIELD,
REUBEN MUSSEY,
SAMUEL WILKINS,
} *Selectmen.*

It will be remembered that at the time this paper was signed many of the young, active men of the town were in the army, doing what the signers pledged themselves to do; hence their names do not appear on this paper.

COMMITTEES OF SAFETY CHOSEN BY THE TOWN DURING THE REVOLUTION.

1776—Josiah Crosby,
William Bradford,
Peter Woodbury,
Thomas Burns,
Robert Means.

1777—Hezekiah Lovejoy,
Stephen Peabody,
Nathaniel Howard,
Josiah Crosby,
John Bradford.

1778—John Bradford,
John Seaton,
Hezekiah Lovejoy,
Oliver Carlton,
Timothy Smith.

1779—John Bradford,
Oliver Carlton,
Hezekiah Lovejoy,
James Hartshorn.

1780—Robert Means,
Hezekiah Lovejoy,
Amos Flint.

1781—James Woodbury,
William Peabody,
William Hogg,
William Bradford, Jr.

The articles of confederation between the several colonies were agreed to by by the citizens of Amherst at a town-meeting, held January 27, 1778.

POPULATION OF AMHERST.

May 13, 1747. Thirty-five families,—fifty-eight men above sixteen years old. Whole population about two hundred and twenty-five.

In a census taken in 1767, the population is classified as follows:

Boys, from 16 years old and under,	200
Unmarried men between 16 and 60 years,	63
Married men " "	135
Men above 60 years,	17
Unmarried females,	270
Married females,	147
Widows,	18
Slaves—males, 6; females, 2,	8
Males, 421; females, 437; total,	858

September 13, 1770, a portion of Monson, containing about eight thousand three hundred acres, with the inhabitants thereon, was annexed to Amherst.

In 1775 the population, as shown by a census taken by order of the state authorities, was 1,428. The original returns of this census are missing.

In 1790 the population by the U. S. census was 2,369.

January 11, 1794, Milford was incorporated: the south-west parish, containing about 80 families, became a part of that town.

In 1800, by the U. S. census, the population of the first parish was 1470; of the north-west parish, 680; total, 2,150,

December 15, 1803, the town of Mont Vernon, containing about 700 inhabitants, taken wholly from Amherst, was incorporated.

1810—United States census,	1,554
1820— " "	1,623
1830— " "	1,657
1840— " "	1,565
1850— " "	1,613
1860— " "	1,508
1870— " "	1,353

OUR FATHERS—THEIR FAITH AND THEIR PRACTICE:

WITH A

TERRITORIAL HISTORY OF THE FIRST PARISH,

AND AN ACCOUNT OF THE

FIRST CHURCH IN MILFORD, FORMERLY AMHERST.

BY WILLIAM B. TOWNE.

After God had carried us safe to New England, and we had builded our houses, provided necessaries for our livelihood, reared convenient places for God's worship, and settled the civil government, one of the next things we longed for and looked after was to advance learning, and perpetuate it to posterity.* Such was the polity of the early settlers. With a country poor, and the people few in number, we find a college† established, and

---

* New England's First Fruits, London, 1643. Mass. Hist. Coll. I, p. 242.

† In the autumn of 1636, only six years from the first settlement of the Massachusetts colony, the General Court voted £400, equal to a tax for one year upon the entire settlement, towards the erection of a public school or college, of which £200 was to be paid the next year, and £200 when the work was finished. In 1638 the Rev. John Harvard, a consumptive, who had been in the country a year or two, died, leaving £779 17s. 2d., one half of his estate, and his entire library, consisting of three hundred and twenty volumes, towards the erection of a college. In that day of small things this bequest was a large sum, and in March, 1639, it was ordered that the college should be called Harvard college, in honor of its benefactor. The first person who had charge of the institution was Nathaniel Eaton—a very unfortunate appointment. He was accused of ill-treating the students, of giving them bad and scanty diet, of exercising inhuman severities towards them, and of beating his usher, Nathaniel Briscoe, in a most barbarous manner. As a result, the court dismissed him from office, fined him one hundred marks (£66 13s. 4d.), and ordered him to pay £30 to Briscoe. He was then excommunicated by the church at Cambridge, soon after which he went to Virginia, from thence to England, where he became a violent persecutor of the Nonconformists, was at length committed to prison for debt, and there ended his days. But this misfortune neither checked the zeal nor dampened the ardor of the earnest men who had the work in charge. *Pierce's History of Harvard University.*

a little later, an enactment "to the end that learning may not be buried in the graves of our forefathers, every township, after the Lord hath increased them to the number of fifty householders, shall appoint one to teach all children to write and read; and where any town shall increase to the number of one hundred families, they shall set up a Grammer school,—the masters thereof being able to instruct youth, so far as they may be fitted for the University."* Here we have a distinct recognition of the idea of education for the whole people. In these measures, says the historian,† "especially in the laws establishing common schools, lies the secret of the success and character of New England. Every child, as it was born into the world, was lifted from the earth by the genius of the country, and in the statutes of the land received, as its birthright, a pledge of the public care of its morals and its mind."

Within thirty years of their settlement we find this people surveying land, and laying out farms in the valley of the Souhegan, regarding it as within their province. And such a conclusion was not strange. Gosnold, Pring, Waymouth,‡ and Smith,‖ of Virginia fame,—an escaped Turkish slave, whose life seems to have belonged more to a mythical age than to that century,—with others of less celebrity in the mother country, had explored the coast, its bays and its rivers; but of the interior but little

---

* Colonial Laws 74, 186.

† Bancroft's History of the United States, vol. 1, p. 459.

‡ Waymouth entered the Penobscot or Kennebec river, and in a shallop, brought in pieces out of England, ascended not much less than three score miles, and kidnapped and carried away five of the natives. "One, standing before, carried our box of merchandise, as we were wont when I went to traffic with them, and a platter of pease, which meat they loved; but before we were landed, one of them, being so suspiciously fearful of his own good, withdrew himself into the wood. The other two met us on the shore side to receive the pease, with whom we went up the cliff to their fire, and sat down with them; and while we were discussing how to catch the third man that was gone, I opened the box and shew them trifles to exchange, thinking thereby to have banished fear from the other, and draw him to return. But when we could not we used little delay, but suddenly laid hands upon them, and it was as much as five or six of us could do to get them into the light horseman (boat); for they were strong, and so naked as our best hold was by their long hair on their heads." Mass. Hist. Coll., vol. 28, p. 144-5.

‖ Smith made a rude map of the coast, superior, perhaps, to any that had preceded it, and was the first to give the country the name of New England. He declared that "truth was more than wealth, and industrious subjects more available to a king than gold."

was known. The marvellous accounts of the explorers, and the religious condition of the country favored colonization; and between 1621 and 1631, including both years, there were not less than twenty charters granted for the purpose of settlement or commerce on the coast of New England.* The grant of Capt. John Mason, in 1622, extended on the coast from where the waters of the Naumkeag discharge themselves into the ocean to the river Merrimack, extending inland to the sources of these streams. The same year Mason and Sir Ferdinando Gorges obtained a grant from the Merrimack to the Kennebec river, bounded by the ocean, and extending back to the great river of Canada. In 1628 Sir Henry Roswell and others received a grant, in width from three miles north of the Merrimack river to three miles south of the Charles, bounded on the Atlantic, and extending back to the western ocean; and it was under this grant that the Massachusetts settlers held their possessions.

The next year, 1629, John Mason received a grant extending "from the middle of Piscataqua river and up the same to the farthest head thereof, and from thence north-westward, until sixty miles from the mouth of the harbor were finished; also through Merrimack river to the farthest head thereof, and so forward up into the land westward until sixty miles were finished; and from thence to cross overland to the end of the sixty miles accounted from the Piscataqua river; together with all islands within five leagues of the coast." † Now it is obvious that grants so profuse and inconsistent could not all stand, and out of the two last mentioned grew the controversy between New Hampshire and Massachusetts, which lasted nearly a century, and was renowned for its acrimony and bitterness. A generation passed away, a new generation took it up, and thus it was carried along till terminated by royal authority. I have already stated that within thirty years of their arrival the inhabitants of the Massachusetts colony were surveying land and laying out farms in the valley of the Souhegan. Within the period mentioned, settlements had extended up to Groton and Chelmsford. From 1655 to 1665 the country was at peace with

* Palfrey's History of New England, vol. 1, pp. 397-8.

† Farmer's edition of Belknap, p. 8.

the aborigines, and the tide of population rolled onward rapidly. In addition to those on the Souhegan, grants were made on both sides of the Merrimack river, on the Nashua river, on Salmon brook, on Penichuck pond, on Penichuck brook, and in other localities, and, with their continuance, the grantees, and those who desired to settle on the farms granted, felt the need of the privileges and immunities of an incorporated township. In accordance therewith, in 1673, they petitioned the General Court and were incorporated, the township being named Dunstable,* and deriving its name from Dunstable in England, some of the proprietors being from that place. It must have been something like fifteen miles from its eastern to its western boundary, and more than twelve miles from its northern to its southern, as it embraced the city of Nashua, the towns of Hudson, Hollis, Tyngsborough, all of Amherst that lies south of the Souhegan, all of Milford on the same side of that river, except a strip a mile in width on the west side of the town, contiguous to the towns of Wilton and Mason, all of Merrimack on the same side of the same river, most of the town of Litchfield, and portions of the towns of Londonderry, Pelham, Brookline, Pepperell, and Townsend. At this time the north-western corner of the county of Middlesex, Massachusetts, was on the south bank of the Souhegan river, a few rods below the bridge recently erected east of the Pine Valley Corporation, and the county maintained its jurisdiction till 1741, when the boundary line between Massachusetts and New Hampshire was determined, severing Dunstable, and bringing about two thirds of the township

---

*The following year the plantation was surveyed and its boundaries were as follows: "It lieth upon both sides Merrimack river on the Nashua river. It is bounded on the south by Chelmsford, by Groton line, and partly by country land. The westerly line runs due north until you come to Souhegan river, to a hill called Dram-cup hill, to a great pine near to the said river at the north-west corner of Charlestown school farm, bounded by Souhegan river on the north; and on the east side of the Merrimack it begins at a great stone which was supposed to be near the north-east corner of Mr. Brenton's farm, and from thence it runs south-south-east six miles to a pine tree marked F, standing within sight of Beaver brook; thence it runs two degrees west of south four miles and a quarter, which reached to the south side of Henry Kimball's farm at Jeremie's hill; thence from the south-east angle of said farm it runs two degrees and a quarter westward of the south near to the head of the long pond which lieth at the head of Edward Colburn's farm. And thus it is bounded by the said pond and the head of said Colburn's farm, taking in Captain Scarlett's farm so as to close again; all of which is sufficiently bounded and described.—*Proprietor's Records.*

within the jurisdiction of New Hampshire. This was very distasteful to many; nevertheless, with the settlement of the province line there was an improved condition of things.

Confidence was strengthened, the tide of settlers moved onward, real property was in demand, and with the increase of population petitions were numerous for a division of the New Hampshire part of old Dunstable. Accordingly, in April, 1746, the legislature of New Hampshire divided it, incorporating the new town of Dunstable,* also Hollis, Merrimack, and

MONSON.

This last named town embraced within its limits most of the present populous part of Milford on the south side of the Souhegan river, all of Amherst on the same side of that river, and a portion of the north-west part of Hollis. Col. Joseph Blanchard† was authorized to call the first meeting of the inhabitants, which was held May 1, only thirty days after the date of the act of incorporation. At a subsequent meeting, held on the 27th of the same month, Col. Joseph Blanchard, James Wheeler, and Robert Colburn were chosen a committee "to make the bound between the town of Hollis and the town of Monson." At the same meeting it was also voted "that there be a pound created and built near to the house of William Nevins upon the most convenient piece of ground." The following petition from the inhabitants was presented to the general assembly of New Hampshire, under date of May 13, 1747. "The petition of the inhabitants of the town of Monson, hereto subscribers, humbly

---

*In 1837 the name was changed to Nashua. In 1842 the town was divided, and the north portion incorporated by the name of Nashville. In 1853 Nashville and Nashua were consolidated and chartered as the city of Nashua.

†Col. Joseph Blanchard was son of Capt. Joseph and Abiah (Hassell) Blanchard; was born at Dunstable Feb. 11, 1704; married Rebecca Hubbard; was an accomplished land surveyor, and for several years was agent of the Masonian proprietors; was in 1740, by mandamus, appointed one of the councillors of New Hampshire, which position he sustained till his death; commanded a regiment in the French war, and was in 1755 stationed at Fort Edward, Washington county, New York, one company of his command being the famous Rogers rangers; was also judge of the superior court from 1749 to 1758. He died April 7, 1758, and his widow April 17, 1774. They had thirteen children, among whom was Augustus Blanchard, Esq., who died in Milford in 1809, having been clerk of the south-west parish ten years, town clerk for the first ten years after the town was incorporated, and a representative of the town to the general court.

sheweth, that the said town is lately begun to settle, and but about fifteen families there; that they are one of the frontier towns west of Merrimack river, and the most northerly one already incorporated lying between Hollis and the new plantation called Souhegan West; that could we be assisted by soldiers, such competent number as might enable us to defend ourselves, shall cheerfully endeavor to stay there, by which we shall serve as a barrier in part to Hollis, Merrimack, and Dunstable; that the last year we were favored by soldiers from Massachusetts* that prevented our drawing off; that should the war be pursued by the enemy as vigorously as last year (unless we are favored by some assistance from the government), we humbly apprehend it would be too great presumption to venture ourselves and families there; that it will be very ruinous to your petitioners to leave their settlements and the frontier widened, and for a necessary defence will require a greater number of soldiers than to assist us there. Wherefore your petitioners pray that a guard for two garrisons and a small scout on our front may be granted to us. James Wheeler, William Nevens, William Colburn, Robert Colburn, Jonathan Taylor, Samuel Leman, Samuel Leman, jr., Abraham Leman, Thomas Nevens, Benjamin Hopkins, Isaac Farwell, Stephen Haselton, John Burns, Thomas Murdow."

Upon the foregoing petition, and a similar one from Souhegan West, the assembly gave orders for enlisting or impressing fifteen good effective men, under proper officers, to scout and guard Souhegan West and Monson till the twenty-third day of October next if need be, and that said men be shifted once a month.

In 1748, Dunstable, Merrimack, Hollis, Nottingham, and Monson united in the choice of a representative to the general assembly, the session to be holden at Portsmouth on the third day of the next January. The town this year voted to raise £60 old tenor for the use of highways, "one half to be done in June, at twenty shillings per day for a man and eight shillings per day

---

*It seems from the tenor of this petition that Massachusetts granted military aid to this infant settlement five years after it had been adjudged within the jurisdiction of New Hampshire.

for a pair of oxen; the other half to be done in September, at fifteen shillings per day for a man, and the same price as in June for a pair of oxen."

In 1749 the annual meeting was at the house of Mr. Thomas Nevins. The fifth article in the warrant was "to see if the town will agree to tax the lands within the whole township for the use of preaching." At the meeting the town voted to dismiss this article. At the same meeting a road two rods wide was laid out from opposite Souhegan bridge, commonly called Lyon's bridge,* up the river through the farms of Madam Tailer, Col. Joseph Blanchard, Benjamin Hopkins, and others.†

1750. At the annual meeting this year, Benjamin Hopkins, Robert Colburn, and Nathan Hutchinson were chosen a committee to adjust the boundary line between Monson and Hollis, and the town again declined to tax the lands within the whole township for the support of preaching.

1751. "Voted that the road from Nathan Hutchinson's land to Mr. Hopkins' house be discontinued, or shut up for a time, without the inhabitants please to put up good gates or good handy bars."

1753. At the annual meeting this year the second article in the warrant was "to see if the town would raise a sum of money for a school; the third, to see if it would tax the lands for building a meeting-house; and the fourth, to raise money for the support of highways,"—all of which articles were decided in the negative. The boundary line between the town and Hollis seems not to have been settled, as at this meeting the matter was referred to the selectmen.

The following petition, in substance, was presented to the general assembly of New Hampshire by the selectmen:— "Whereas, the inhabitants of Monson have received a late order to render into the office of the secretary of state an invoice of their polls and estates in order for apportioning the

---

*In the early settlement of the country the bridge over the river near the Amherst railroad station was called Lyon's bridge, and derived its name from Ebenezer Lyon, who lived near it as early as 1748, and who died in 1798, aged 88 years.

† Widow Abagail Tailer, of Boston, at this time owned a farm of 300 acres in the neighborhood of the East Milford railroad flag station, Col. Joseph Blanchard another between that and where the present village in Milford is now located, and Benjamin Hopkins owned the Charlestown school farm.

taxes, which we have done, and would further beg leave to remonstrate our infancy and inability to bear any part of the public burden at present; that there is but thirty-six polls in the whole, several of them being transiently hired to labor for a short space of time; that there are but twenty-one houses, chiefly small cottages, only for a present shelter, the charge of building yet to come; that the householders are all plain men, dwelling in tents, husbanding their employments, their improvements very small, their lands unsubdued, their progress much retarded by their necessity to work out of town during the prime of the year, or at other business to procure provisions, and, though the town is a part of old Dunstable, it has till now been a portion and remained a total wilderness; that till within a few years the owners were under no obligation to settle the lands that were very recently granted to gentlemen in farms, by which means the few settlers are scattered all about the town, and that much labor has and must be spent in opening and making roads, bridges, &c., that are of present necessity a burden too heavy for the small, weak number that is there; that in the late war they were at the expense of garrisoning, scouting, and defending themselves, besides many other charges they must have and must go through; so therefore apprehend themselves utterly unable to bear any part of the public taxes as yet; but hope their small beginning in time may become useful, if they may be nursed and favored now in their infancy. Wherefore your petitioners pray that they may be considered in their infant and chargeable state, and that they may not be taxed till they are of ability to go through their own necessary charge, and when that shall be, they will cheerfully contribute according to their power."

1754. This year John Shepard,* William Peabody, Andrew Bradford, Israel Towne, Archelaus Williams, Richard Gould, Thomas Williams, John Hutchinson, John Edmonds, and others,

---

* John Shepard then resided within the present limits of the village in Milford, on the north side of Souhegan river, where Mr. John Marvell now lives; William Peabody on the old Peabody farm, farther up the river on the same side, late the property of the late T. T. Farnsworth and Israel Towne, within the present limits of Amherst, on the farm owned by Abel and Frank W. Chase. The prayer of the petitioners would have annexed to Monson a strip of territory about seven miles in length by two in width, and would have included nearly the whole of Amherst plain.

petitioned the governor and council to be annexed to Monson. They represented themselves substantially as inhabitants of a tract of land north of and adjoining Monson, lying within no incorporation, town, or district; that the town of Monson is situated in length, east and west, near eight miles, in breadth but about four miles, and is bounded on the northerly side by Souhegan river, both sides of which river are generally fruitful and profitable land for corn and grass; that if the town of Monson were enlarged on the north so as to add and include the following tract of land—beginning at the north-east corner of Monson, on Souhegan river, and running north by the line of Merrimack two miles, then begin the west station at the north-west corner of Monson and run thence north two miles, then in a straight line to the end of the two miles first mentioned—which would be an addition of about seven thousand acres, and would make the town about five and one half miles in width generally; that the said river is small; that many bridges are now and must continue to be kept in repair, so that the river is no inconvenience to this union; that it will be for the accommodation of Monson, and that several of the petitioners have for many years been settled here, and have made their improvements at heavy expense; that they have not had the benefit of any incorporation in any town, nor do they see any present prospect of incorporation unless they are annexed to Monson.

1755. At the annual meeting this year the question of taxing the land for building a meeting-house was again agitated, and again decided in the negative.

1756. At this annual meeting the question was again raised, and again decided in the negative, and an effort to raise a sum of money for a school part of the year was also decided in the negative. Before the close of the year, however, a special meeting was called to fix upon a place for locating the meeting-house, and it was decided to set it in the most convenient place, near the centre of the town.*

1758. The annual meeting this year was held at the house of Archelaus Towne, innholder. The third article in the warrant

* Tradition points to a locality on the northerly slope of Duncklee hill as the place fixed upon, and it still retains the name of "the meeting-house lot."

was "to see if the town will vote to tax the lands of residents and non-residents for building a meeting-house," which question at the meeting was decided in the negative. The fifth article in said warrant was "to see if the town will come into any agreement with Capt. Shepard concerning the one half of his bridge, or allow him some satisfaction for the same." On this article it was voted to allow Capt. Shepard some satisfaction for one half of his bridge, and James Wheeler, Benjamin Herrick, and Nathan Hutchinson were chosen a committee to adjust the matter. At a subsequent meeting this year it was voted to raise £250 old tenor for the use of highways, £70 to pay Capt. Shepard for one half of his bridge over the river at his mill, and £16 to William Jones for plank put on said bridge. The £250 for highways was never raised, the inhabitants at a later meeting reconsidering the vote.

1759. The town again voted not to tax the lands for building a meeting-house. Chose William Jones and Josiah Crosby to inspect the deer.

1760. Voted to petition the governor and council of the province to set off or annex the land on the south side of Monson to Hollis, and to annex such part of Souhegan West to the remainder of Monson as will be sufficient to maintain the gospel, and other charges incident to towns.

1761. Voted to raise £100 old tenor to defray town charges; declined to tax the lands for building a meeting-house; voted to grant the petition of Hollis that a mile and one half, or thereabouts, be set off agreeable to the petition of said Hollis; and dismissed the article relative to fixing a place to locate the meeting-house.

1763. Benjamin Hopkins, John Burns, Joseph Gould, John Burns, jr., Thomas Burns, and George Burns, at the annual meeting, protested against a division of the town. The voters, however, sustained their former position; also, voted to raise £300 old tenor for the support of preaching, each person to pay their money where they hear.

1764. Voted to sink the £300 old tenor raised last March for the support of preaching. The fourth article in the warrant this year was "to see if the town would agree to build a meeting-house, and fix upon a place to set it," which article was decided in the negative. The fifth was "to see if the town would raise a sum of money to hire preaching," which was also decided in the negative. The sixth was "to see if the town would raise a sum of money in order to make satisfaction to the towns of Hollis and Amherst for the privilege of worshipping with them." For this purpose it was voted to raise £400 old tenor. The seventh article was "to see if the town would provide one or more burial-places in the town," which article was dismissed. The tenth article was "to see if the town would be at the charge of making another road where Mr. Benjamin Hopkins has flowed the town road, or take a course of law with him for damages." Upon this article the town voted to take a course of law, and appointed the selectmen to prosecute the suit. On the 12th of September this year another town meeting was held, at which it was voted to build a meeting-house, to petition the general court for a tax upon the lands of residents and non-residents for building the same, and Benjamin Hopkins, Nathan Hutchinson, and Josiah Crosby were chosen a committee to carry the matter to the general court.

1765. At the annual meeting this year the fourth article in the warrant was "to see if the town will vote to tax the lands of residents and non-residents to build a meeting-house and settle a minister, and if not, to nullify and make void the former vote for that purpose." The proposition to erect a meeting-house and settle a minister was not sustained. The town this year voted to raise £250 old tenor to defray town charges.

1767. The town voted this year that the money raised in the year 1764, and assessed for the towns of Hollis and Amherst, should not be collected.

1769. The town declined to raise money for the support of highways.

1770. On the ninth day of April a special meeting was called, when it was voted that the town be divided between Hollis and Amherst, both of these towns having assented to the arrangement. The division was as follows, viz.: Beginning at the north-east corner of Monson, and running south by the line of Merrimack two miles, then due west to the west line of Monson, then north to Souhegan river, then down said river to the bound first mentioned to be annexed to Amherst, the remainder to Hollis. By this arrangement Amherst acquired its first territory on the south side of the Souhegan river. The reason assigned for a division in the petition of Monson* to the governor and council was, "that the land in and about the centre of said Monson is so very poor, barren, broken, and uneven, as cannot admit of many settlers, so that those families that are in town are almost all planted in the extreme parts of it. We therefore conceive that if a division were made, as above mentioned, the interest and good of the people in it would be much promoted thereby, especially as we have no prospect of ever building a meeting-house, in the centre or elsewhere, any way, to accommodate us, by which difficulty we think the gospel will not be settled amongst us while in the present situation." Thus was Monson blotted out, after an existence of twenty-four years. For the last twelve years of her continuance, her annual

---

*TOWN CLERKS AND SELECTMEN OF THE TOWN OF MONSON.

	Town Clerk.	*First Selectman.*	*Second Selectman.*	*Third Selectman.*
1746.	Robert Colburn,	Benjamin Hopkins,	Robert Colburn,	William Nevins.
1747.	Robert Colburn,	Benjamin Hopkins,	Robert Colburn,	William Nevins.
1748.	Robert Colburn,	Robert Colburn,	Benj. Hopkins,	Samuel Leman.
1749.	Robert Colburn,	Benjamin Hopkins,	Robert Colburn,	Samuel Leman.
1750.	Robert Colburn,	Benjamin Hopkins,	Robert Colburn,	Nathan Hutchinson.
1751.	Robert Colburn,	Robert Colburn,	William Nevins,	Nathan Hutchinson.
1752.	Robert Colburn,	Benjamin Hopkins,	Robert Colburn,	William Nevins.
1753.	Robert Colburn,	Benjamin Hopkins,	Robert Colburn,	Benjamin Farley.
1754.	Robert Colburn,	Benjamin Hopkins,	Robert Nevins,	William Nevins.
1755.	Robert Colburn,	Benjamin Kenrick,	Robert Colburn,	William Nevins.
1756.	Benjamin Kenrick,	Benjamin Kenrick,	John Brown,	William Jones.
1757.	Robert Colburn,	Robert Colburn,	Benjamin Kenrick,	John Brown.
1758.	Robert Colburn,	Robert Colburn,	John Brown,	William Nevins.
1759.	Benjamin Kenrick,	Benjamin Kenrick,	Jonathan Taylor,	Thomas Nevins.
1760.	Benjamin Kenrick,	Robert Colburn,	Benj. Hopkins,	Benjamin Kenrick.
1761.	Benjamin Kenrick,	Benjamin Kenrick,	William Nevins,	Nathan Hutchinson.
1762.	Benjamin Kenrick,	Nathan Hutchinson,	William Nevins,	Robert Colburn.
1763.	Benjamin Kenrick,	Benjamin Kenrick,	Daniel Kenrick,	Josiah Crosby.
1764.	Robert Colburn,	Robert Colburn,	Nat'n Hutchinson,	William Nevins.
1765.	Benjamin Kenrick,	Benjamin Hopkins,	William Nevins,	Benjamin Kenrick.
1766.	Benjamin Kenrick,	Benjamin Kenrick,	William Nevins,	Nathan Hutchinson.
1767.	Archelaus Towne,	Archelaus Towne,	Robert Colburn,	Josiah Crosby.
1768.	Archelaus Towne,	Archelaus Towne,	Josiah Crosby,	Daniel Kenrick.
1769.	Archelaus Towne,	Archelaus Towne,	Joseph Gould,	Thomas Burns.
1770.	Benjamin Kenrick,	Benjamin Kenrick,	William Nevins,	Josiah Crosby.

meetings were held at the house of Archelaus Towne,* innholder.

She had no public structure except a pound. She resolutely refused to raise money for the support of schools, and while she occasionally, at a special meeting, voted in favor of the first steps towards public religious instruction, at her annual meetings she invariably negatived such vote. A century has passed since her demise, and but for the recent finding† of a portion of her records, but few persons of to-day would know that she ever existed.

1771. The harmony that prevailed last year, when annexation was so popular, was not of long continuance, for in January of this year about thirty of the most prominent of those that were last year annexed petitioned the governor and council for a division of Amherst. They recite in their petition,—"That the town of Amherst is about nine miles in length, by reason that about half the town of Monson was of late annexed to it, and is capable of being divided into two towns or parishes without prejudice to or spoiling the same; that many of us live in that part of Amherst which was lately Monson, and our being annexed to said Amherst was contrary to our desire and interest; that we are so remote from the centre of Amherst that it is, and ever will be, with great expense, inconvenience, and difficulty to us and our families to attend public worship, by reason of the distance; that many of our estates are not so valuable by reason of our being annexed to Amherst, for before that our

*Archelaus Towne, son of Israel and Grace (Gardner) Towne, was born at Topsfield, Mass., in 1734; came to Souhegan West with his father at the age of about six years; married Martha, born July 24, 1737, daughter of Ephraim Abbott. They resided in Monson, at what is now known as Danforth's Corner, in Amherst, where he kept a tavern for several years. They had seven children. His wife died in 1773, after which he raised a company, took command of it, joined the continental army, and died at Fishkill, N. Y., in November, 1779. He was a man large of stature, of great physical strength and power of endurance, fond of the hardship and excitement of frontier life, a natural leader, and one that commanded the confidence of his associates.—Narrative of Jonathan Towne, who died at Milford Dec. 31, 1842, in the 89th year of his age.

†The Hon. Samuel T. Worcester, of Nashua, being engaged in the preparation of an article upon the early history of Hollis, was informed by his brother, the Hon. John N. Worcester, of Hollis, that there formerly existed, in the town clerk's office of that town, records relating to Monson. This led the former to procure the nearly worn out volume, have what remained of it bound, and put in condition to prevent further immediate waste.

situation was nigh the centre of Monson, and on that account purchased our lands at a dear rate, and Monson being annihilated, our situation is more inconvenient than before."

Amherst followed with a counter petition, in which it was stated,—"That for more than twenty years last past a number of persons living on those lands lately known by the name of Monson, but more lately joined to Amherst, not having a minister settled among them nor accommodation sufficient for that purpose, as they said, very constantly attended the worship of God with us in said Amherst, not doing anything with us towards our meeting-house, nor towards the support of our minister, except some small private donations made to our minister. However, they repeatedly requested our town to consent to receive them, promising to meet at any place that the major part of the people should fix to build a house on, whereupon our town, after repeated solicitations to receive them, gave their consent. And your excellency and honors, some time in July last, saw fit to aggregate about one half of said Monson to said Amherst. Soon after, our town saw it necessary to build a meeting-house, and voted to do it, our present meeting-house being small and insufficient for the old town and said new addition. The most of the people of the new addition were present, and some voted in the affirmative, some in the negative; but they began to think that the charter subjected them to the same duties with us of the old town, that they must defray some part of the charges of building and so forth, and not only so, but must do something towards supporting our minister. These reflections affected some of them very sensibly. They had not been acquainted with anything of the kind. They were ready to construe it as a degree of persecution and the like. And to remedy this evil they are about petitioning to have our town, as it now lies, divided into two parishes, which we think can not be done without a manifest injury to more than three quarters of the town. A very considerable quantity of land in our town is barren and poor, and will not admit of two parishes; besides, it lies in such a situation by reason of a river and hills, that the whole of the people may more conveniently meet at one place, the place pitched upon, than at any two places in the town."

No action was taken by the state authorities upon either of these petitions, and quiet seems to have been restored. The new meeting-house was built and dedicated, the worshippers gathered in this new sanctuary from all parts of the town, and the continuous exercises of yesterday and to-day, after the lapse of a century, are a fitting recognition of that event.

THE SOUTH-WEST PARISH.

In the year 1782 forty-seven persons, as follows, viz.,

Nathan Hutchinson,
Andrew Bradford,
Josiah Crosby,
Sampson Crosby,
James Gilman,
Thomas Burns,
Isaac Abbott,
Elisha Hutchinson,
Benjamin Hutchinson,
Josiah Crosby, Jr.,
John Wallace,
Stephen Crosby,
Augustus Blanchard,
John Burns,
William Crosby,
John Bradford,
Thaddeus Grimes,
Israel Burnham,
John Grimes,
Nathan Hutchinson, Jr.,
Bartholomew Hutchinson,
David Burnham,
Arthur Graham,
Samuel Graham,
William Wallace,
Ebenezer Averill,
Moses Averill,
Joshua Burnham,
Stephen Burnham,
Jonathan Hutchinson,
Abner Hutchinson,
William Peabody,
Elijah Averill,
Ebenezer Hopkins,
Jonathan Grimes,
George Burns,
William Grimes,
Darius Abbott,
Samuel How,
Jonathan Towne,
Henry Codman,
William Melendy,
Samuel Dodge,
Bartholomew Towne,
Benjamin Hopkins, Jr.,
Benjamin Conant,
Benjamin Hopkins, 3d,

were constituted the third or south-west parish in Amherst, "for transacting ministerial affairs only." The reason assigned by the incorporators for the formation of this parish was, that their local situation rendered it impracticable for some of them and many of their children to give a general attendance at the stated place of public worship, and, further, that they conceived they could well be spared, there being about three hundred ratable polls taxed to the first parish. There was no boundary to the new parish, neither were the members exempt from former obligations, one condition being, that nothing in its organization should be construed to exempt any of said parishioners, their polls or estates, from paying their just proportion of all ministerial charges already arisen in said town of Amherst, nor from the future support, according to contract, of the Rev. Daniel Wilkins, the late minister of said town then living.* The date of incorporation was November 23, and the first meeting was held at the house of Thaddeus Grimes, on the fourteenth day of the next January. At this meeting Capt. Nathan Hutchinson† was chosen moderator; Augustus Blanchard, clerk and treasurer; Augustus Blanchard, Lieut. Thomas Burns, and Capt. John Bradford, assessors; and Benjamin Hutchinson, collector;—and it was "voted to build a meeting-house of the same size and bigness the north-west parish hath built, except the porches," and that Lieut. Darius Abbott, Capt. Josiah Crosby, and Capt. Andrew Bradford be a committee to provide timber, boards, and shingles, and let the same out at public vendue to the lowest bidder." At the first annual meeting of the parish, holden at the house of Thaddeus Grimes, innholder, on the fourth day of March, 1783, it was voted to raise £32 4s. to discharge the expense of the parish being set off, £95 to be laid out in purchasing timber, boards, shingles, and other materials for building the meeting-house, £15 to pay for preaching the current year, and that Capt Nathan Hutchinson, Lieut. Thomas Burns, and Capt. John Bradford be a committee to hire preaching. Later in the same year another meeting was called to

*The Rev. Daniel Wilkins at this time was aged and infirm, had been settled upwards of forty years, and lived only three months after the formation of this parish, dying February 11, 1783, in the seventy-third year of his age.

† Capt. Nathan Hutchinson, a very active and efficient man in town and parish affairs, was son of Benjamin and Sarah (Tarbell) Hutchinson, of Bedford, Middlesex county, Mass., and married Rachel Stearns. In 1744 he purchased of Benjamin Hopkins one hundred acres of land, near the centre of the Charlestown school farm,—bounded north by the river, south by the south line of said farm, of equal width at each end, also bounded by a black oak on Saddle hill. He came here from Billerica in June, 1748, located on Elm street, where E. D. Searles now resides, and died June 12, 1795, aged 78 years. His widow died on the 25th of July, in the same year, aged 76 years.

make choice of a place where the meeting-house should be erected, and make provision for clearing the same. After adjourning from the house of Mr. Grimes to the place regarded as the most desirable location, it was voted that the house should stand about twenty rods south of Shepard's bridge, on a rise of ground. This vote would have located the meeting-house on what are now the premises of Doctor S. S. Stickney. At a meeting held still later this year, Capt. Nathan Hutchinson, John Wallace, and John Burns were chosen a committee to procure stone for underpinning the meeting-house, and Joshua Burnham was authorized to purchase a "parish book."

At the annual meeting, holden March 2, 1784, it was voted to proceed with the meeting-house, and to begin to frame it the first Monday in June, and raise it as soon as possible. Capt. Nathan Hutchinson, Capt. Josiah Crosby, and Capt. Andrew Bradford were chosen a committee to see that the meeting-house is framed, underpinned, and raised. It was also voted to raise £30 towards the expense of the meeting-house—£20 to pay for preaching; that three shillings per day be allowed each man for work on the meeting-house,—the laborer to board himself; and that any person who shall hereafter join the parish, shall be exempt from any tax raised, to raise, board, and shingle the meeting-house. For some reason, not discernible at this time, the location that had been fixed upon did not prove satisfactory, for, at a special meeting held on the 15th day of June, it was decided that it should be located about ten rods north-west from the former place, between two pitch pine stumps; that Augustus Blanchard, Lieut. Thomas Burns, Joshua Burnham, Capt. John Bradford, and Lieut. Benjamin Hutchinson, be a committee to carry on the work, and that said committee provide one barrel of rum, two barrels of cider, and one quarter of sugar for the raising. Thus, it would seem that the meeting-house was raised in the summer of 1784, for, on the second day of September of this year, a special meeting was called, and the second article in the warrant was to see if the parishioners would board, shingle, or finish any part of the meeting-house frame,—when it was voted to board and shingle it; that it be boarded with square edged boards, and that the boarding and shingling be let to the lowest bidder at vendue. At the same meeting, it was voted to raise

£40 to defray the expense of furthur finishing the meeting-house; and Lieut. Thomas Burns and Lieut. Darius Abbott were chosen a committee to wait upon Governor Hopkins, and get the donation he hath offered to procure the nails. It was common among our ancestors in England, and continues to the present time, of denominating the chief man, or the man at the head of prominent movements or establishments, as the governor;* and the title, in this case, must have been derived in this way. In 1659, the general court of Massachusetts granted to the town of Charlestown 1,000 acres of land, from the unappropriated lands of the province, for the support of a school. The next year it was surveyed by that celebrated land surveyor, Jonathan Danforth, of Billerica, and described thus:—"Laid out, for the use of the school of Charlestown, one thousand acres of land, more or less in the wilderness, on the western side of Merrimack river, at a place commonly called by the Indians, Sowheaganucke, beginning at the foot of a great hill, and so extending eastward about two miles down said river, and bounded by the river on the north, and by land laid out for Mrs. Anna Cole on the east, the wilderness elsewhere surrounding according to marked trees, all of which are sufficiently bounded with C, and is more fully demonstrated by a platt taken of the same." † The title of Indians was extinguished by deed, dated July 14, 1671.‡ The north-west corner of this tract of land was on the south bank of the river, a few rods below the new bridge at Jones's crossing, and was identical with the north-west corner of Old Dunstable, the north-west corner of Middlesex county, Massachusetts, for more than sixty years, and the north-west corner of the late town of Monson. This tract extended down the river to the present east line of the farm of William Ramsdell, and no more attractive piece of land of the same magnitude exists in this region. The town of Charlestown continued to own it till May, 1743, when it was purchased by Benjamin Hopkins, of Billerica, for £375, and as early as 1745 he resided on it. A saw-mill is a necessity in a new settlement, and he early built

---

* The translators of the Bible observed it, in James 3:4.

† Mass. General Court Records.

‡ Middlesex County Registry of Deeds.

one upon Whitehall brook, a little west of where the house of Moses Proctor now stands; and, if any one will proceed into the field, about fifty rods northerly of the house of Luke Smith, to a little point of land on the border of the brook, overlooking the river and the intervale, and remove the turf, he will occasionally find in the soil a small piece of brick or stone that has once been in a chimney, a wall, or a fire-place, indicating that a dwelling once stood there. It was on this spot in the wilderness, with nothing to guide him but marked trees, that Mr. Hopkins erected his bullet-proof dwelling—a kind of fort, built of timber, to protect himself and family from the fierce beasts of the forest, and fiercer men. On the north side of the river lived William Peabody, John Shepard, and Israel Towne; on the south side his nearest neighbor was in the west parish of Dunstable, now Hollis; and his oldest son married Anna Powers, the first white child born in that town.* Such is a brief outline of one who had, by universal consent, acquired the title of Governor,† and who, after a residence of upwards of forty years in the neighborhood, was making a donation to purchase the nails for the new meeting-house. At a subsequent meeting, in November, it was voted to provide clapboards, door-steps, boards for the lower floor, sashes, suitable stuff for window-frames, and glass, and that Capt. Nathan Hutchinson, Capt. William Peabody, and Capt. Josiah Crosby be a committee to provide the materials voted, and see that they are delivered at the meeting-house.

At the annual meeting holden on the 1st day of March, 1785, it was voted to raise £50 to be laid out on the meeting-house, and to raise £30 to hire preaching and defray parish charges. On the 7th day of the same month there was a special meeting called, and the second article in the warrant was to see if the parishioners will build porches to the meeting-house, or let any person or persons build the same for the ground the same may save in the house. At this meeting it was voted to build porches, and a committee was chosen for that purpose,

---

* Narrative of the venerable John Hopkins in 1840.

† He died June 11, 1787, aged 85 years; and his widow died July 30, 1792, aged 93 years.

8

and instructed to have the work done as soon as the other outside work on the house was completed. At the same meeting William Peabody, Benjamin Hopkins, and Joshua Burnham were chosen a committee to hire preaching the current year. At another special meeting, held on the 25th of April, Nathan Hutchinson, Augustus Blanchard, and Thomas Burns were chosen a committee to sell the pew-ground in the meeting-house, at public vendue, to the highest bidder, and give proper conveyances to the purchasers, and that the money arising from the sale be laid out in further finishing the meeting-house. It was also voted to put in all the joist and braces in the meeting-house not already in, and that John Burns be allowed 23 shillings lawful money for doing the same.

A still further special meeting was held on the 5th of September, when it was voted to lay the lower floor, and to let the same out at vendue to the lowest bidder, and it was struck off to Thomas Boynton at thirty-nine shillings. Thomas Burns, Nathan Hutchinson, and John Wallace were chosen a committee to procure proper floor nails, see that the sills were properly underpinned, and the floors laid in a good workmanlike manner. On the 25th day of December, another special meeting was held, when it was decided to have the sashes, window-frames, doors, body seats, and stuff for the body seats, put up at vendue, to be bid off by the lowest bidder. Nathan Hutchinson, Caleb Jones, and Josiah Crosby were chosen a committee to vendue the work off, to procure at the expense of the parish all the necessary materials for doing the work, and to see that it was done in a good workmanlike manner,—the work to be completed by the first day of next June. The sashes were bid off by Thomas Boynton, at 15s. 2d. old tenor; the window frames, by David Chandler at 8s. 11d.; front door, by Benjamin Conant at 20s.; the body seats and stuff for the same, by Nathan Hutchinson.

A warrant was issued for an annual meeting to be held on the 7th day of March, 1786; the fourth article therein being to see if the parishioners would finish the outside of the meeting-house or any part thereof; and the fifth was to see if they would have the £40, voted at the last annual meeting to be laid out on the meeting-house, assessed and collected; but the records contain no reference to this meeting. There was, however, a special meeting held on the fourth of September in this year, when it was voted to accept the plan of Temple meeting-house porches and build in the same form, and also voted to procure glass and glazing materials for the meeting-house. At the annual meeting in March, 1787, there was no allusion to the meeting-house, but £30 was voted for the support of preaching. At a meeting in September of this year, a committee was chosen to get the glass set, and the sashes put in the window-frames, and £10 was voted to set the front-door steps, clear round the meeting-house, and level the ground before said house.

The year 1788 was an eventful one in parish affairs. William Crosby gave the parish the following described pieces of land, viz.: "Beginning at the south-west corner of Shepard's bridge, thence running southerly on the west side of the road leading from said bridge to my house,* until it comes to the main road that leads from my house to Wilton, to a stake and stones; from thence westerly on the north side of said road about eight rods to a white oak stump; thence northerly to a black oak tree marked, standing on the bank of Souhegan river; from thence by said river to the place of beginning, being the land the meeting-house stands on. Also, one other piece, to be appropriated for a burying-ground, on the west part of my farm, bounded as follows, viz.: Beginning at a large white pine tree standing on the bank of the river a few rods north of the ditch bridge (so called); from thence east thirteen rods to a stake and stones; from thence south twelve rods to a stake and stones; from thence west until it comes to the river; and from thence by the river to the bound first mentioned, containing about one acre." These were parts of a tract of land of 500 acres granted in October, 1659, by the General Court of Massachusetts to Mrs. Anna Cole. The record reads thus: "In consideration of the liberal gifts to the country in the will of

---

*The first house erected on Union square—was raised in 1783, was occupied early in the present century by Dr. Robert Fuller, was known for many years as the old Fuller house, stood where the town hall now stands, and was removed to make room for that structure.

Capt. Robert Keayne,* the whole court met together and voted," &c. At the date of the grant she was the widow of Capt. Keayne, but the next year became the wife of Samuel Cole. This tract was bounded on the north by the river 350 rods, and extended from the west line of the present farm of Matthias F. Crosby on Elm street down the river, near to the steam-mill of David Heald. In 1780, Josiah Crosby, in consideration of three hundred bushels of grain, two thirds Indian corn and one third rye, purchased 113 acres in the north-east corner of this tract, extending on the river from near the steam-mill, before mentioned, up a little above the west corner of the old cemetery. In 1782 he sold the same to his son William, and in the first of these conveyances it is referred to as part of the tract belonging to Mather Byles.†

---

*Robert Keayne, merchant of London, came over in the ship Defence in 1635, aged 40 years, with his wife Ann, aged 38 years, and son Benjamin, aged 16 years. He is characterized by Winthrop as "a man of eminent parts, an ancient professor of the gospel, coming over for its advancement and for conscience' sake, as wealthy, given to hospitality, very useful to the country, and a large contributor to its free schools." He was one of the founders and the first captain of the Ancient and Honorable Artillery Company, was four times a representative of the town of Boston, and once speaker of the House of Deputies. Notwithstanding his virtues and usefulness, he became obnoxious on account of selling dearer than the law allowed, for which offence, after solemn trial, he was convicted and fined £250. His will occupies 148 folio pages of the probate records of Suffolk county, Massachusetts, in which he vindicates his character with a pathos indicative of a keen sense of the injustice to which he had been subjected, adding "that though he had suffered enough from the public to tie up both his hands, yet being desirous to requite evil with good, and though he cannot forget, being willing to forgive, and deeming it a want of gratitude to God for prosperous men to leave all to wife, children, or relatives, and nothing to the public or to charity," he proceeds to give £1200 to objects of public use or private charity, included in which were £250 to Harvard college.

†Mather Byles was born in Boston, March 26, 1706, and on his mother's side was descended from Richard Mather and John Cotton ; was graduated at Harvard University, in 1725, and ordained the first pastor of Hollis Street church in 1733. His first wife was a niece of Governor Belcher, the second a daughter of Lieutenant-Governor Tailer, and it is probable this land came to him by inheritance. He continued his pastorate till 1776, when, on account of disloyalty, the connection was dissolved and never renewed. The next year he was denounced in town meeting, subsequently tried, found guilty of attachment to the royal cause, sentenced to confinement, and with his family to be sent to England. This sentence was never enforced, and he died in Boston, July 5, 1788, having received the degree of D. D. from Aberdeen University in 1765.

He was distinguished among his contemporaries for his wit, his solid learning, and his excellent literary taste. Pope, Lansdowne, and Watts were his correspondents, and many of his witticisms have come down to us. On one occasion, when required to remain in his house under guard, he persuaded the sentinel to go on an errand for

The month following the gift of the land, the parish voted "to ceil round the meeting-house as high as the windows; to case, make, and hang the end-doors, lay the platforms for the pews on the lower floor, and case the lower windows;" and the south-west corner, from the front to the west door, including the west door, ceiling, casing, and laying the platforms, was let to Joshua Burnham for 39s.; the south-east corner, from the front door to the east door, including the east door, the ceiling, casing, and laying the platforms, was let to Josiah Crosby for 41s.; from the east door to the west door round the north side, the ceiling, casing, and laying the platforms was let to John Wallace for 51s.; the platforms for the pews in the inside square was let to Jotham Shepard for 19s., the work being let by vendue to the lowest bidder, the boards and nails for all the work and the hinges for the doors to be found by the parish. At a special meeting called in September, the parish further voted to finish the whole meeting-house; and Augustus Blanchard, Thomas Burns, and Josiah Crosby were chosen a committee of the pew-ground in the galleries, and lay the same before the parish on the 29th inst., to which time the meeting was adjourned. At the adjourned meeting, the plan of the committee was accepted, and they were authorized to sell the pews at public vendue to the highest bidder, and apply the proceeds to the further finishing of the house; and as it might be necessary to give the committee further instructions, the meeting adjourned to the 13th of October. At this meeting the pews were sold, and the stuff and material for finishing the house "vendued" to the following persons, they being the lowest bidders, namely,—to Josiah Crosby, jr., 2 M laths at 7s. each, and 1 M feet merchantable boards at 18s.; Augustus Blanchard, 2 hhds. lime at 24s. 6d. each; Joseph Wallace, 2 M laths at 7s. each; Stephen Crosby, 3 M laths at 7s.,

---

him, promising to perform sentinel's duty in his absence. To the great amusement of his neighbors he gravely marched before his own door with musket on his shoulder till his keeper returned, and when inquired of in relation to his occupation, said he was guarding Mather Byles. After his trial, in alluding to the fact that he had been put under guard, the guard removed, and then again replaced, he observed that he had been guarded, re-guarded and disregarded. In 1780, on the celebrated dark day, a lady who resided near the doctor sent her young son to him to know if he could account for the uncommon appearance. His reply was, "Give my compliments to your mamma, and tell her I am as much in the dark as she is."

1 M feet boards at 18s., and 2 hhds. lime at 24s. each; Isaac Abbott, 2 M laths at 7s. each, 3 hhds. lime at 24s.; Andrew Bradford, jr., 1 M laths, 7s.; Caleb Jones, 1 M feet 1¼ in. white pine boards, 1 M feet inch do.—do. clear stuff for the work intended; Daniel Johnson, 1 M feet merchantable boards, 18s.; Josiah Osgood, 1 M do., 18s., 2 corner girths, 12 by 14 inches; Joshua Crosby, one half M white pine boards for ceiling, 9s.; Jacob Hale, 500 feet pine plank 2 in. thick 14 in. wide, 16s.; 100 feet pine plank, 3 in. thick, 14 in. wide, at 4s.; 400 slitwork, 3 by 4 in., at 8s., and hhd. lime, 25s.; hewed white pine timber, 6 by 7 in., suitable length for the gallery breast-work, sills for the seats and studs at 8s. 6d.; Thomas Burns, 2 hhds. lime, 25s. each.

In December the parish voted to agree with Mr. Thurston or some other minister to preach six months during the year next ensuing.

At the annual meeting, in 1789, it was voted to raise £36 to pay for preaching and defray parish expenses; that twelve feet in the front of the gallery be appropriated for a pew for the singers; that ten pounds be laid out in work round the meeting-house, " and that John Burns, Caleb Jones, and Benjamin Conant be a committee to see the work done. In October it was voted to enlarge the singers' pew, and that it be seventeen feet, and no longer." At the annual meeting, the next year, it was voted to build and sell two pews of six feet front each, at each end of the singers' pew in the gallery, and that the pews be built at the expense of the parish.

In January, 1791, at a special meeting, the question of having the parish set off by lines was agitated, and a committee was appointed to treat with the first parish for the following lines, viz.,—" Begin at the north-east corner of Ebenezer Averill's land, and running southerly, including Andrew and John Bradford's intact, William Peabody's, the widow Shepard, Jotham and Daniel Shepard and John Shepard, Esq., until it comes to Souhegan river, then down said river to Merrimack west line, including all belonging to Amherst, on the south side of said river." At the annual meeting this year, it was voted to raise £40 to pay for preaching, and to defray parish expenses; but there was nothing in the warrant relative to the parish being "set off by lines." In June, however, a special meeting was called, when not only the question of the parish being set off by lines was agitated, but the question of being set off as a separate town was considered, and it was voted to petition the General Court, as soon as may be, to be set off by lines or a separate town; and a committee, consisting of Joshua Burnham, Josiah Crosby, Augustus Blanchard, Thomas Burns, and Porter Lummus, were appointed for that purpose, and £12 appropriated to pay their expenses.*

At the annual meeting, in 1792, it was voted to raise £60 to pay for preaching, and defray parish expenses, and in June, of this year, the parish was incorporated, by the name of the southwest parish, in Amherst, and boundaries fixed thereto. In October, it was voted to sell the remaining pews at public vendue, apply the money arising from such sale to the painting and further finishing the meeting-house, and a committee was appointed to give a title to the pews sold. At the annual meeting, the next year, the parish voted to raise £55 to pay for preaching, and to defray parish expenses, and that the funds of former collectors be applied "to the further finishing and painting the meeting-house."

Thus we see that it took upwards of ten years of continuous struggle for the parishioners to complete their house of worship, —a struggle that we of to-day can scarcely comprehend. Nearly forty years since, a venerable man then living, one of the founders of the church and an active worker in this enterprise, was asked by the speaker what year the meeting-house was completed, to which he replied, "We scarcely knew when it was completed ourselves, for at no time during the work did we have any clear conception of what would constitute a finished house. We worshipped in Col. Shepard's barn,† and when the meeting-

*The parish not only took this step to be set off, but in October, 1793, voted to petition the General Court in connection with the mile slip, Duxbury school farm, and a part of Hollis, to be set off as a separate town, and in Jan., 1794, these several parcels of territory were made a separate town, and incorporated by the name of Milford.

† To us, worshipping in the comfortable if not luxurious houses of to-day, holding a meeting in a barn seems an absurdity,—yet an inquiry into the practices of the early settlers shows that this was no uncommon thing; and a sermon preached in the barn of Major Cole, of Mont Vernon, by Rev. Mr. Coggin, of Chelmsford, Mass., upon the importance of building a meeting-house in that parish, was an effective instrumentality in accomplishing that work.

house was so far finished that we could hold meetings in it, we thought we had accomplished a great work. We were poor, our means necessarily limited, frequently divided in council, and nothing but the privilege, for ourselves and our children, of worshipping God in his sanctuary could have held us together and induced us to complete the work." Truly was it said yesterday, in the excellent historical discourse to which most of us listened, "people do not move into the forests, clear for themselves homesteads in the solitudes of the wilderness, and take on themselves the burden of building meeting-houses and sustaining ministers, without deep convictions of the value of the gospel."

CHURCH ORGANIZED.

The church in this parish, denominated the third church in Amherst, was organized by an ecclesiastical council, Nov. 19, 1788.* The council consisted of Jonathan Livermore,† Abiel Fiske,‡ John Bruce,‖ Moses Putnam, Ebenezer Rockwood, Richard Ward, Daniel Mansfield, and William Bradford.

In the proceedings of the council twelve persons are named as constituting the church, viz.:

---

*The churches organized in Hillsborough county, previous to the commencement of the present century, are as follows:—

	Organized.		Organized.		Organized.
Nashua,	1685	Wilton,	1763	Hancock,	1788
Hudson,	1737	Hillsborough,	1769	Milford,	1788
Amherst,	1741	Goffstown,	1771	Weare,	1789
Litchfield,	1741	Temple,	1771	Deering,	1789
Hollis,	1743	Merrimack,	1772	Greenfield,	1791
Pelham,	1751	Mason,	1772	Brookline,	1796
Lyndeborough,	1757	Francestown,	1773	Peterborough,	1799
New Ipswich,	1761	Mont Vernon,	1780		

†Rev. Jonathan Livermore, a native of Northborough, Worcester county, Mass., born in 1739, was graduated at Harvard college in 1760; was the first minister of Wilton, being ordained there in 1763. He sustained the pastoral relation in that place about fifteen years, when he was dismissed, but did not leave town, remaining till his death, which occurred July 20, 1809, aged 79 years.

‡Rev. Abel Fiske was born at Pepperell, Mass., May 28, 1752; was graduated at Harvard college in 1774; taught the Grammar school, and studied divinity at Concord, Mass.; was ordained at Wilton in November, 1778, and was pastor of the church till his death, which took place April 21, 1802, at the age of 50 years.

‖Rev. John Bruce, the first minister in Mont Vernon, was born at Marlborough, Mass., in 1757; entered Dartmouth college at the age of about twenty years; was graduated in 1781; was settled in 1785, and continued his pastorate till his death, which occurred March 12, 1809.

Stephen Burnham,	Thomas Burns,
Caleb Jones,	Jonathan Towne,
Elisha Hutchinson,	Benjamin Conant,
John Wallace,	Benjamin Hutchinson,
Joseph Wallace,	William Melendy,
Nathan Hutchinson,	Jonathan Jones.

Attached to the covenant are seven additional names, viz.:

James Wallace,	Letitia Wallace,
Hannah Bradford,	Mary Wallace,
Mary Burnham,	Betsy Wallace.
Sarah Hutchinson,	

The first meeting was held at the house of William Crosby * soon after the organization, when Elisha Hutchinson was chosen Clerk, which office he held till his death.† At this meeting an examining committee was chosen, and it was decided that applicants for admission might relate their religious experience verbally or in writing, and that no persons should be admitted who would not come up to the standard of full communion. The next year several meetings were held, but they related solely to the discipline of a member. Then follows a period of nearly six years in which no meeting seems to have been held, at the expiration of which time the church and town concurred in giving "Mr. Kiah Bailey" a call, the vote in the joint body being forty-nine for, and thirty against. Subsequently, the

* William Crosby, the benefactor of the parish,—whose house seems to have been open for parish, church, and other meetings, whenever business vital to the welfare of the body politic was to be considered,—was a descendant of Simon Crosby, aged 26 years, who, with his wife Ann, aged 25 years, and their son Thomas, aged 8 weeks, and came to this country in the ship Susan and Ellen in 1635 ("Founders of New England," page 22), settled in Cambridge, near where Harvard college is now located, and was the son of Josiah and Sarah (Fitch) Crosby, who came here from Billerica in 1753, and located on the opposite side of the road near where the late Frederic Crosby lived. He was born Jan. 29, 1758; married Sarah, daughter of John Shepard; and died esteemed and respected, May 12, 1831, aged 73 years. His younger brother Asa, who was born July 15, 1765, and who died at Hanover, April 12, 1836, was the father of Hon. Nathan Crosby of Lowell, Dr. Josiah Crosby of Manchester, the late Dr. Dixi Crosby of Hanover, Prof. Alpheus Crosby of Salem, and the late Prof. Thomas Russell Crosby of Hanover.

† Elisha Hutchinson, grandfather of the famous "Hutchinson family" of vocalists, was the son of Joseph and Hannah (Richardson) Hutchinson; was born at Middleton, Essex county, Mass., Dec. 6, 1751; married Sarah, daughter of Amos and Mary Buxton of Danvers; settled here, in 1779, on the farm, in the north part of the town, now in possession of Dodge G. Hartshorn, and died Oct. 12, 1800, aged 49 years.

town non-concurred in the movement. The next year, 1796, the church and the town concurred in giving Mr. Phineas Randall a call to settle with them in the work of the ministry, but Mr. Randall did not accept. Then follows a period of nearly two years, when no meeting was held, after which Rev. Abel Fiske, of Wilton, was elected Standing Moderator, and a committee chosen to give information to the members whenever a church meeting should be appointed by the moderator. About this time the town voted, seventy-six to thirty-one, to give Mr. Nath'l H. Fletcher* a call, but the church did not concur. At this time the church had been organized nearly ten years, but its existence must have been merely nominal. It could only have lived in name, as no deacons had been chosen, nor members admitted either by letter or by the profession of their faith, and there is no record indicating that a communion season had been observed. In March, 1798, the question of receiving members by letters from other churches was considered, and in April it was decided in the affirmative, and nineteen members were thus received, five being from the church in Amherst, two from the second church in Amherst, six from the church in Wilton, three from the church in Billerica, two from the church in Dracut, and one from the church in Durham. It was also voted at the same meeting to have the sacrament of the Lord's Supper administered twice during the coming season, and two persons were appointed to wait on the table. Two additional persons were also chosen for the purpose of conversing with those who should apply for admission, and the moderator was instructed to call a meeting at any time, at the request of any seven members. In August, 1799, a meeting was held to consider the question of giving Mr. Micah Stone a call, but it

---

*Nathaniel Hill Fletcher, son of Deacon Abel and Abigail (Hildreth) Fletcher, was born at Boxborough, Middlesex county, Mass., April 16, 1769; was graduated at Harvard University in 1793; received the honorary degree of A. M. at Brown University in 1799; was settled at Wells, Me., in 1800; was married February 8, 1801, to Sarah, daughter of John Storer, of the same place; and, after a ministry of 27 years, resigned his pastorate and returned to Boxborough, where he died Sept. 4, 1834. Several of his sermons were published, among which was one delivered at Deerfield, in this state, in 1812, at the ordination of Rev. Nathaniel Wells; a Thanksgiving sermon, delivered in Massachusetts, in November of the same year; one delivered at the funeral of Rev. Paul Coffin, D. D., of Buxton, Me., June 8, 1821; and one on Christian communion, in 1827.

was regarded as inexpedient. In the year 1800 the church, fifteen of the nineteen members present, voted to invite Mr. Thomas Beede to become their pastor, and the town concurred, proposing $566 as a settlement to be paid within one year after the ordination, an annual salary of $333 while he supplied the desk, and $110 annually during his residence in town, after he should be unable to supply the desk; and the next year a unanimous call of the church was extended to Mr. Joshua Lane. It would be interesting at the present time to know what were the hindrances to the settlement of the various candidates, and how the matter in each case was treated by the parties in interest; but the records are silent on the subject.

In March, 1802, the church, nineteen members being present, invited Rev. Humphrey Moore to settle with them in the gospel ministry. The town concurred, in April, and chose a committee of fifteen to determine what settlement and salary was proper to offer Mr. Moore for his services in the ministry. This committee, after the consideration of the matter for one hour, reported $600 as a settlement to be paid, or to become due in one year after the ordination, $400 as an annual salary, and a gratuity of $100 per annum while he should remain their minister, and be unable, through infirmity or old age, to supply the desk. In August, Mr. Moore gave an answer in the affirmative, and on the 13th day of the following October he was ordained, the exercises on the occasion being,—

1. Anthem.
2. Introductory Prayer, by Rev. Ebenezer Hill, of Mason.
3. Sermon, Luke ix, 60, by Rev. Elijah Dunbar, of Peterboro'.
4. Ordaining Prayer, by Rev. Jacob Burnap, of Merrimack.
5. Charge, by Rev. Jeremiah Barnard, of Amherst.
6. Concluding Prayer, by Rev. Lemuel Wadsworth, of Brookline.
7. Benediction by the pastor.

With the settlement of the new pastor, a brighter day dawned upon the church. The month following, a confession of faith was adopted, deacons chosen,* and stated communion seasons

* Moses Towne and Benjamin French were chosen, neither of whom accepted, and at the next meeting, holden in May, 1803, John Wallace and William Lovejoy were chosen, and entered upon their duties.

agreed upon; steps indicating faithful, earnest work. At the time of the ordination, the church had been in existence about fourteen years, but had had no additions except on one occasion, and then by letter. The subsequent year witnessed the membership doubled, thirty-two being added on profession of their faith, and seven by letters from other churches.

Of the pastorate of Mr. Moore, extending over a third part of a century, I need not speak.* It is in part if not in whole within the memory of many present. The 335 additions to the church during his ministry testify to the diligence and faithfulness of his labors, and are evidence of consecration to his chosen work. And in conclusion, let me add that, in what I have said to-day, I have endeavored to let the fathers speak in their own language, revealing their characters in their own words, supplying no motives, and purposely abstaining from comments, that we might, unprejudiced, commend what was commendable and noble in their lives; and if, amid their trials, their sufferings, and sacrifices, we discovered mistakes in method, what was little in character, or want of devout affection for one another, it might be earnestly deplored, and avoided in our own experience.

---

*Rev. Humphrey Moore was dismissed March 9, 1836; remained in the parish, and died April 8, 1871, in the 93d year of his age. The following named pastors have succeeded him:—

Rev. J. W. Salter was installed April 27, 1836; dismissed Oct. 24, 1838.
Rev. Abner B. Warner was ordained Feb. 6, 1839; dismissed Oct. 27, 1846.
Rev. Lycurgus P. Kimball was installed May 19, 1847; dismissed Aug. 7, 1849.
Rev. E. N. Hidden was installed Nov. 21, 1849; dismissed April 7, 1858.
Rev. S. C. Kendall was installed April 7, 1858; dismissed Oct. 15, 1860.
Rev. F. D. Ayer was ordained May 1, 1861; dismissed Sept. 8, 1867.
Rev. Geo. E. Freeman was installed Dec. 23, 1868; dismissed Dec. 14, 1871.
Rev. George Pierce, Jr., was installed Oct. 29, 1872.

www.ingramcontent.com/pod-product-compliance
Lightning Source LLC
LaVergne TN
LVHW021421110826
845150LV00007B/2026

* 9 7 8 1 4 2 5 5 0 8 9 0 6 *